The Conference of the Birds

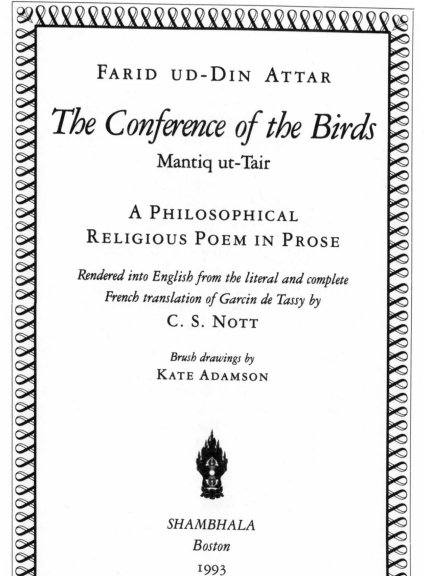

FARID UD-DIN ATTAR

The Conference of the Birds
Mantiq ut-Tair

A PHILOSOPHICAL
RELIGIOUS POEM IN PROSE

*Rendered into English from the literal and complete
French translation of Garcin de Tassy by*
C. S. NOTT

Brush drawings by
KATE ADAMSON

SHAMBHALA
Boston
1993

Shambhala Publications, Inc.
Horticultural Hall
300 Massachusetts Avenue
Boston, Massachusetts 02115

9 8 7 6 5 4 3 2 1

Printed in the United States of America on acid-free paper ∞
Distributed in the United States by Random House, Inc., and in
Canada by Random House of Canada Ltd

Library of Congress Cataloging-in-Publication Data

Aṭṭār, Farīd al-Dīn, d. ca. 1230. [Manṭīq al-ṭayr. English]
The conference of the birds: a Sufi fable/Farid ud-Din Attar;
translated by C. S. Nott. p.   ISBN 0-87773-031-8 (pbk.)
    1. Sufi poetry, Persian—Translations into English.
I. Nott, C. S. II. Title. PK6451.F4M2813   1993
      891'.5511—dc20   92-56447 CIP

CONTENTS

FOREWORD

Attar's great philosophical religious poem, Mantiq Uttair, *was composed probably in the second half of the twelfth century A.D. Since then, a new edition has appeared every few years in one or another of the countries of the Near East.*

The present rendering was undertaken in the first instance for the benefit of myself and some friends; but it is the fullest version that has yet appeared in English and, as such, may interest a wider public. For the most part I have used Garcin de Tassy's translation into French prose from the Persian, which was collated with Arabic, Hindu, and Turkish texts (Paris, 1863). I have also consulted a Persian text through a Sufi friend, together with extant English translations. Of these latter there are three, all very much abridged. The first is by Edward Fitzgerald, in rhyme, and rather sentimental; the second is a very literal translation of 1,170 couplets of the original 4,674 Mathnawī, by Ghulam Muhammad Abid Shaikh, India, 1911; the third (and the best of the three) is Masani's, in prose, though only about half of the original was translated; this was printed and published in Mangalore, India, 1924, and sheets were imported and published by the Oxford University Press. All three have long been out of print. Garcin de Tassy's translation is complete, and, as he says, 'is as literal as I have been able to make it intelligible'. He has also retained the flavour, the spirit, and the teaching of Attar's poem.

I have omitted the second half of the Invocation—which is missing from the Hindu text and is abridged in the Turkish. The Epilogue is omitted entirely from the Hindu and the Turkish texts, and varies in other manuscripts; of this I have included only the first part, since the rest, consisting as it does of anecdotes, comes as an anticlimax. Also omitted or condensed are a few anecdotes in the story, either because they seem repetitive, or because the meaning is obscure. But all that relates to the 'Conference', 'Speech', 'Language', 'Dis-course' or 'Parliament' (as it is variously called) of the Birds as told in the original manuscript, is here.

All notes on the text are included in the Glossary so that the reading shall not be interrupted; these include some of Tassy's. In compiling this, and in writing the notes on Attar and on the Sufis, I have consulted, among other sources, The Dictionary of Islam *and the* Encyclopaedia of Islam. *In numbering the sections I have followed Tassy's translation of the original manuscripts. If the reader will run through the Glossary before reading the book many allusions will be made clearer; though, as Tassy himself remarks, the meaning is sometimes obscure.*

Miss Adamson's brush drawings are based on those in an old Persian manuscript of Mantiq Uttair.

C. S. NOTT

The Conference of the Birds

I. INVOCATION

PRAISE to the Holy Creator, who has placed his throne upon the waters, and who has made all terrestrial creatures. To the Heavens he has given dominion and to the Earth dependence; to the Heavens he has given movement, and to the Earth uniform repose.

He raised the firmament above the earth as a tent, without pillars to uphold it. In six days he created the seven planets and with two letters he created the nine cupolas of the Heavens.

In the beginning he gilded the stars, so that at night the heavens might play tric-trac.

With diverse properties he endowed the net of the body, and he has put dust on the tail of the bird of the soul.

He made the Ocean liquid as a sign of bondage, and the mountain tops are capped with ice for fear of him.

He dried up the bed of the sea and from its stones brought forth rubies, and from its blood, musk.

To the mountains he has given peaks for a dagger, and valleys for a belt; so that they lift up their heads in pride.

Sometimes he makes clusters of roses spring from the face of the fire;

Sometimes he throws bridges across the face of the waters.

He caused a mosquito to sting Nimrod his enemy who thereby suffered for four hundred years.

In his wisdom he caused the spider to spin his web to protect the highest of men.

He squeezed the waist of the ant so that it resembled a hair, and he made it a companion of Solomon;

He gave it the black robes of the Abbasides and a garment of unwoven brocade worthy of the peacock.

When he saw that the carpet of nature was defective he pieced it together fittingly.

He stained the sword with the colour of the tulip; and from vapour made a bed of water-lilies.

He drenched clods of earth with blood so that he might take from them cornelians and rubies.

Sun and Moon—one the day, the other the night, bow to the dust in adoration; and from their worship comes their movement. It is God who has spread out the day in whiteness, it is he who has folded up the night and blackened it.

To the parrot he gave a collar of gold; and the hoopoe he made a messenger of the Way.

The firmament is like a bird beating its wings along the way God has marked out for him, striking the Door with his head as with a hammer.

God has made the firmament to revolve—night follows day and day the night.

When he breathes on clay man is created; and from a little vapour he forms the world.

Sometimes he causes the dog to go before the traveller; sometimes he uses the cat to show the Way.

Sometimes he gives the power of Solomon to a staff; sometimes he accords eloquence to the ant.

From a staff he produces a serpent; and by means of a staff he sends forth a torrent of water.

He has placed in the firmament the orb of the proud, and binds it with iron when glowing red it wanes.

He brought forth a camel from a rock, and made the golden calf to bellow.

In winter he scatters the silver snow; in autumn, the gold of yellow leaves.

He lays a cover on the thorn and tinges it with the colour of blood.

To the jasmine he gives four petals and on the head of the tulip he puts a red bonnet.

He places a golden crown on the brow of the narcissus; and drops pearls of dew into her shrine.

At the idea of God the mind is baffled, reason fails; because of God the heavens turn, the earth reels.

From the back of the fish to the moon every atom is a witness to his Being.

The depths of earth and the heights of heaven render him each their particular homage.

God produced the wind, the earth, the fire, and blood, and by these he announces his secret.

He took clay and kneaded it with water, and after forty mornings placed therein the spirit which vivified the body.

God gave it intelligence so that it might have discernment of things.

When he saw that intelligence had discernment, he gave it knowledge, so that it might weigh and ponder.

But when man came in possession of his faculties he confessed his impotence, and was overcome with amazement, while his body gave itself up to exterior acts.

Friends or enemies, all bow the head under the yoke which God, in his wisdom, imposes; and, a thing astonishing, he watches over us all.

At the beginning of the centuries God used the mountains as nails to fix the Earth; and washed Earth's face with the water of Ocean. Then he placed Earth on the back of a bull, the bull on a fish, and the fish on the air. But on what rested the air? On nothing. But nothing is nothing—and all that is nothing. Admire then, the works of the Lord, though he himself considers them as nothing. And seeing that His Essence alone exists it is certain there is nothing but Him. His throne is on the waters and the world is in the air. But leave the waters and the air, for all is God: the throne and the world are only a talisman. God is all, and things have only a nominal value; the world visible and the world invisible are only Himself.

There is none but Him. But, alas, no one can see Him. The eyes are blind, even though the world be lighted by a brilliant sun. Should you catch even a glimpse of Him you would lose your wits, and if you should see Him completely you would lose your self.

All men who are aware of their ignorance tuck up the flap of their garment and say earnestly: 'O thou who art not seen although thou makest us to know thee, everyone is thou and no other than thou is manifested. The soul is hidden in the body, and thou art hidden in the soul. O thou who art hidden in that which is hidden, thou art more than all. All see themselves in thee and they see thee in every-thing. Since thy dwelling is surrounded by guards and sentinels how can we come near to thy presence? Neither mind nor reason can have access to thy essence, and no one knows thy attributes. Because thou art eternal and perfect thou art always confounding the wise. What can we say more, since thou art not to be described!'

O my heart, if you wish to arrive at the beginning of understanding, walk carefully. To each atom there is a dif-ferent door, and for each atom there is a different way which leads to the mysterious Being of whom I speak. To know oneself one must live a hundred lives. But you must know God by Himself and not by you; it is He who opens the way that leads to Him, not human wisdom. The knowledge of Him is not at the door of rhetoricians. Knowledge and ignorance are here the same, for they cannot explain nor can they describe. The opinions of men on this arise only in their imagination; and it is absurd to try to deduce anything from what they say: whether ill or well, they have said it from themselves. God is above knowledge and beyond evidence, and nothing can give an idea of his Holy Majesty.

O you who value the truth, do not look for an analogy; the existence of this Being without equal does not admit of one. Since neither the prophets nor the heavenly messengers have understood the least particle, they have bowed their foreheads on the dust, saying: 'We have not known thee as thou must truly be.'

What am I then, to flatter myself that I know Him?

O ignorant son of the first man, the Khalif of God on earth, strive to participate in the spiritual knowledge of your father. All creatures that God draws out from nothingness for their existence prostrate themselves before him. When he wished to create Adam, he made him go out from behind a hundred veils, and he said to him, 'O Adam, all creatures adore me; be adored in your turn.' The only one who turned from this adoration was transformed from an angel into a demon. He was cursed and had no knowledge of the secret. His face became black and he said to God: 'O thou who art in possession of absolute independence, do not abandon me.'

The Most High replied: 'You who are cursed, know that Adam is both my steward and the king of nature. Today go before him, and tomorrow burn for him the ispand.'

When the soul was joined to the body it was part of the all: never has there been so marvellous a talisman. The soul had a share of that which is high, and the body a share of that which is low; it was formed of a mixture of heavy clay and pure spirit. By this mixing, man became the most astonishing of mysteries. We do not know nor do we understand so much as a little of our spirit. If you wish to say something about this, it would be better to keep silent. Many know the surface of this ocean, but they understand nothing of the depths; and the visible world is the talisman which protects it. But this talisman of bodily obstacles will be broken at last. You will find the treasure when the talisman disappears; the soul will manifest itself when the body is laid aside. But your soul is another talisman; it is, for this mystery, another substance. Walk then in the way I shall indicate, but do not ask for an explanation.

In this vast ocean the world is an atom and the atom a world. Who knows which is of more value here, the cornelian or the pebble?

We have staked our life, our reason, our spirit, our religion, in order to understand the perfection of an atom. Sew up your lips and ask nothing of the empyrean or the throne of God. No one really knows the essence of the atom—ask whom you will. The Heavens are like a cupola upside down, without stability, at once moving and unmoving. One is lost in contemplation of such a mystery—it is veil upon veil; one is like a figure painted on a wall, and one can only bite the back of one's hand.

Consider those who have entered in the way of the Spirit. Look what has happened to Adam; see how many years he spent in mourning. Contemplate the deluge of Noah and all that patriarch suffered at the hands of the wicked. Consider Abraham, who was full of love for God: he suffered tortures and was thrown into the fire. See the unfortunate Ishmael offered up in the way of divine love. Turn towards Jacob who became blind from weeping for his son. Look at Joseph, admirable in his power as in his slavery, in the pit and in prison. Remember the unhappy Job stretched on the earth a prey to worms and wolves. Think of Jonah who, having strayed from the Way, went from the moon to the belly of the fish. Follow Moses from his birth: a box served him for a cradle, and Pharaoh exalted him. Think of David, who made himself a breast-plate and whose sighs melted the iron like wax. Look at Solomon whose empire was mastered by the Jinn. Remember Zacharias, so ardent with the love of God that he kept silent when they killed him; and John the Baptist, despised before the people, whose head was put on a platter. Stand in wonder at Christ at the foot of the cross, when he saved himself from the hands of the Jews. And finally, ponder over all that the Chief of the Prophets suffered from the insults and injuries of the wicked.

After this, do you think it will be easy to arrive at a knowledge of spiritual things? It means no less than to die to everything. What shall I say further, since there is nothing more to say, and there remains not a rose on the bush! O Wisdom! You are no more than a suckling child; and the reason of the old and experienced strays in this quest. How shall I, a fool, be able to arrive at this Essence; and if I should arrive, how shall I be able to enter in by the door? O Holy Creator! Vivify my spirit! Believers and unbelievers are equally plunged in blood, and my head turns as the heavens. I am not without hope but I am impatient.

My friends! We are neighbours of one another: I wish to repeat my discourse to you day and night, so that you should not cease for a moment to long to set out in quest of Truth.

II. THE BIRDS ASSEMBLE

WELCOME, O Hoopoe! You who were a guide to King Solomon and the true-messenger of the valley, who had the good fortune to go to the borders of the Kingdom of Sheba. Your warbling speech with Solomon was delightful; being his companion you obtained a crown of glory. You must put in fetters the demon, the tempter, and having done this will enter the palace of Solomon.

O Wagtail, you who resemble Moses! Lift up your head and make your shawm resound to celebrate the true knowledge of God. Like Moses you have seen the fire from afar; you are really a little Moses on Mount Sinai. My discourse is sans words, sans tongue, sans sound; understand it then, sans mind, sans ear.

Welcome, O Parrot! In your beautiful robe and collar of fire, this collar is fitting for a dweller in the underworld but your robe is worthy of Heaven. Can Abraham save himself from the fire of Nimrod? Break the head of Nimrod and become the friend of Abraham, who was the friend of God. When you have been delivered from the hands of Nimrod put on your robe of glory and fear not the collar of fire.

Welcome, O Partridge! You who walk so graciously, and are content when you fly over the mountains of divine knowledge. Lift yourself up in joy and consider the benefits of the Way. Knock with the hammer on the door of the house of God; and humbly melt down the mountains of your perverse desires so that the camel can come out.

Salutations, O Falcon Royal! You of piercing sight, how long will you remain so violent and passionate? Fasten your talons to the letter of eternal love but do not break the seal until eternity. Mix your spirit with reason and see the eternity of before and after as one. Break your vile carcase

and establish yourself in the cavern of unity, and Muhammad
will come to you.

Salutations, O Quail! When you hear in your spirit the
alast of love, your body of desire replies, balé, with displeasure. Consume your body of desire as the ass of Christ,
then, as the Messiah, enflame yourself with the love of the
Creator. Burn this ass and take the bird of love, so that the
Spirit of God may happily come to you.

Salutations, O Nightingale of the Garden of Love! Utter
your plaintive notes caused by the wounds and pains of
love. Lament sweetly from the heart, like David. Open
your melodious throat and sing of spiritual things. By your
songs show men the true Way. Make the iron of your heart
as soft as wax, and you will be like David, fervent in the love
of God.

Salutations, O Peacock of the Garden of the Eight Doors!
You have been afflicted because of the seven-headed serpent,
through whom you were expelled from Eden. If you deliver
yourself from this detestable serpent Adam will take you
with him into Paradise.

Salutations, O Excellent Pheasant! You see that which
is far off, and you perceive the heart's source immersed in
the ocean of light while you remain in the pit of darkness
and the prison of uncertainty. Lift yourself from the pit and
raise your head to the divine throne.

Salutations, O gently moaning Turtle-dove! You went
out contented and returned with a sad heart to a prison as
narrow as Jonah's. O you who wander here and there like
a fish, can you languish in ill-will? Cut off the head of this fish
so that you may preen yourself on the summit of the moon.

Salutations, O Pigeon! Intone your notes so that I may
scatter round you seven plates of pearls. Since the collar of
faith encircles your neck it would not become you to be
unfaithful. When you enter into the way of understanding,
Khizr will bring you the water of life.

Welcome, O Hawk! You who have taken wing, and after rebelling against your master have bowed your head! Bear yourself becomingly. You are fastened to the body of this world, and so are far from the other. When you are free of the worlds, present and future, you will rest on the hand of Alexander.

Welcome, O Goldfinch! Come joyously. Be eager to act, and come as the fire. When you have burnt up your attachments the light of God will manifest itself more and more. Since your heart knows the secrets of God, remain faithful. When you have perfected yourself you will no longer exist. But God will remain.

III. THE CONFERENCE OF THE BIRDS

I

THE CONFERENCE OPENS

ALL THE BIRDS of the world, known and unknown, were
assembled together. They said: 'No country in the world
is without a king. How comes it, then, that the kingdom of
the birds is without a ruler! This state of things cannot last.
We must make effort together and search for one; for no
country can have a good administration and a good organiza-
tion without a king.'

So they began to consider how to set out on their quest.
The Hoopoe, excited and full of hope, came forward and
placed herself in the middle of the assembled birds. On her
breast was the ornament which symbolized that she had
entered the way of spiritual knowledge; the crest on her
head was as the crown of truth, and she had knowledge of
both good and evil.

'Dear Birds,' she began, 'I am one who is engaged in
divine warfare, and I am a messenger of the world invisible.
I have knowledge of God and of the secrets of creation.
When one carries on his beak, as I do, the name of God,
Bismillah, it follows that one must have knowledge of many
hidden things. Yet my days pass restlessly and I am concerned
with no person for I am wholly occupied by love for the
King. I can find water by instinct, and I know many other
secrets. I talk with Solomon and am the foremost of his

followers. It is astonishing that he neither asked nor sought
for those who were absent from his kingdom, yet when I
was away from him for a day he sent his messengers everywhere, and, since he could not be without me for a moment,
my worth is established for ever. I carried his letters, and I
was his confidential companion. The bird who is sought
after by the prophet Solomon, merits a crown for his head.
The bird who is well spoken of by God, how can he trail his
feathers in the dust? For years I have travelled by sea and
land, over mountains and valleys. I covered an immense
space in the time of the deluge; I accompanied Solomon on
his journeys, and I have measured the bounds of the world.

'I know well my King, but alone I cannot set out to find
him. Abandon your timidity, your self-conceit and your
unbelief, for he who makes light of his own life is delivered
from himself; he is delivered from good and evil in the way
of his beloved. Be generous with your life. Set your feet
upon the earth and step out joyfully for the court of the
king. We have a true king, he lives behind the mountains
called Kāf. His name is Simurgh and he is the king of birds.
He is close to us, but we are far from him. The place where
he dwells is inaccessible, and no tongue is able to utter his
name. Before him hang a hundred thousand veils of light
and darkness, and in the two worlds no one has power to
dispute his kingdom. He is the sovran lord and is bathed in
the perfection of his majesty. He does not manifest himself
completely even in the place of his dwelling, and to this no
knowledge or intelligence can attain. The way is unknown,
and no one has the steadfastness to seek it, though thousands
of creatures spend their lives in longing. Even the purest
soul cannot describe him, neither can the reason compre-
hend: these two eyes are blind. The wise cannot discover
his perfection nor can the man of understanding perceive
his beauty. All creatures have wished to attain to this perfection and beauty by imagination. But how can you tread that

path with thought? How measure the moon from the fish? So, thousands of heads go here and there, like the ball in polo, and only lamentations and sighs of longing are heard. Many lands and seas are on the way. Do not imagine that the journey is short; and one must have the heart of a lion to follow this unusual road, for it is very long and the sea is deep. One plods along in a state of amazement, sometimes smiling sometimes weeping. As for me, I shall be happy to discover even a trace of him. That would indeed be something, but to live without him would be a reproach. A man must not keep his soul from the beloved but must be in a fitting state to lead his soul to the court of the King. Wash your hands of this life if you would be called a man of action. For your beloved, renounce this dear life of yours, as worthy men. If you submit with grace, the beloved will give his life for you.'

FIRST MANIFESTATION OF THE SIMURGH

'An astonishing thing! The first manifestation of the Simurgh took place in China in the middle of the night. One of his feathers fell on China and his reputation filled the world. Everyone made a picture of this feather, and from it formed his own system of ideas, and so fell into a turmoil. This feather is still in the picture-gallery of that country; hence the saying, "Seek knowledge, even in China!"

'But for his manifestation there would not have been so much noise in the world concerning this mysterious Being. This sign of his existence is a token of his glory. All souls carry an impression of the image of his feather. Since the description of it has neither head nor tail, beginning nor end, it is not necessary to say more about it. Now, any of you who are for this road, prepare yourselves, and put your feet on the Way.'

When the Hoopoe had finished the birds began excitedly to discuss the glory of this king, and seized with longing to have him for their own sovereign they were all impatient to be off. They resolved to go together; each became a friend to the other and an enemy to himself. But when they began to realize how long and painful their journey was to be, they hesitated, and in spite of their apparent good-will began to excuse themselves, each according to his type.

2

THE NIGHTINGALE

The amorous Nightingale first came forward almost beside himself with passion. He poured emotion into each of the thousand notes of his song; and in each was to be found a world of secrets. When he sang of these mysteries the birds became silent. 'The secrets of love are known to me,' he said. 'All night I repeat my songs of love. Is there no unhappy David to whom I can sing the yearning psalms of love? The flute's sweet wailing is because of me, and the lamenting of the lute. I create a tumult among the roses as well as in the hearts of lovers. Always I teach new mysteries, at each instant I repeat new songs of sadness. When love overpowers my soul my singing is as the sighing sea. Who hears me forsakes his reason, though he be among the wise. If I am parted from my dear Rose I am desolate, I cease my singing and tell my secrets to none. My secrets are not known to everyone; only to the Rose are they known with certainty. So deep in love am I with the Rose that I do not even think of my own existence; but only of the Rose and the coral of her petals. The journey to the Simurgh is beyond my strength; the love of the Rose is enough for the Nightingale. It is for me that she flowers with her hundred petals; what more then can I wish! The Rose which blooms today is full of longing, and for me smiles joyously. When she shows her face under the veil I know that it is for me. How then can the Nightingale remain a single night deprived of the love of this enchantress?'

3

THE HOOPOE

The Hoopoe replied: 'O Nightingale, you who would stay behind dazzled by the exterior form of things, cease to delight in an attachment so deluding. The love of the Rose has many thorns; it has disturbed and dominated you. Although the Rose is fair, her beauty is soon gone. One who seeks self-perfection should not become the slave of a love so passing. If the smile of the Rose arouses your desire it will only fill your days and nights with lamentations. Forsake the Rose and blush for yourself: for she laughs at you with each new Spring and then she smiles no more.'

THE HOOPOE TELLS THE STORY OF THE PRINCESS AND THE DERVISH

A king had a daughter as beautiful as the moon, who was loved by everyone. Passion was awakened by her sleepy eyes and by the sweet intoxication of her presence. Her face was white as camphor, her hair musk-black. Jealousy of her lips dried up a ruby of the finest water, while sugar melted in them for shame.

By the will of destiny a dervish caught sight of her, and the bread he held dropped from his hand. She passed him like a flame, and as she passed, she laughed. At this the dervish fell in the dust almost deprived of life. He could rest neither by day nor night and wept continually. When he thought of her smile he shed tears as a cloud drops rain. This frantic love went on for seven years, the while he lived in the street with dogs. At last her attendants resolved to put an end to him. But the princess spoke to him in secret and said: 'How is it possible for there to be intimate relations between you and me? Go at once, or you will be killed: don't stay any longer at my door, but get up and go.'

The poor dervish replied: 'The day I fell in love with you I washed my hands of life. Thousands such as I sacrifice themselves to your beauty. Since your men are bent on killing me unjustly, answer one simple question. On the day you became the cause of my death, why did you smile at me?' 'O you fool,' she said, 'when I saw that you were about to humiliate yourself, I smiled from pity. I am permitted to smile from pity but not from mockery.' So saying, she vanished like a wisp of smoke, leaving the dervish desolate.

4

THE PARROT

Then came the Parrot with sugar in her beak, dressed in a garment of green, and round her neck a collar of gold. The hawk is but a gnat beside her brilliance; earth's green carpet is the reflection of her feathers, and her words are distilled sugar. Listen to her: 'Vile men whose hearts are iron have shut me in a cage, so charming am I. Held fast in this prison I long for the source of the water of immortality guarded by Khizr. Like him I am clothed in green, for I am a Khizr among birds. I should like to go to the source of this water, but a moth has not strength to lift itself to the Simurgh's great wing; the spring of Khizr is enough for me.'

The Hoopoe replied: 'O you who have no idea of felicity! He who is not willing to renounce his life is no man. Life has been given to you so that for an instant you may have a worthy friend. Set out upon the Way, for you are not an almond you are only the shell. Join the company of worthy men and enter freely in their Way.'

THE FOOL OF GOD AND KHIZR

There was a man, mad from love of God. Khizr said to him: 'O perfect man, will you be my friend?' He replied: 'You and I are not compatible, for you have drunk long draughts of the water of immortality so that you will always exist, and I wish to give up my life. I am without friends and do not know even how to support myself. Whilst you are busy preserving your life, I sacrifice mine every day. It is better that I leave you, as birds escape the snare, so, good-bye.'

5

THE PEACOCK

Next came the golden Peacock, with feathers of a hundred—what shall I say?—a hundred thousand colours! He displayed himself, turning this way and that, like a bride. 'The painter of the world,' he said, 'to fashion me took in his hand the brush of the Jinn. But although I am Gabriel among birds my lot is not to be envied. I was friendly with the serpent in the earthly paradise, and for this was ignominiously driven out. They deprived me of a position of trust, they, who trusted me, and my feet were my prison. But I am always hoping that some benevolent guide will lead me out of this dark abode and take me to the everlasting mansions. I do not expect to reach the king you speak of, it will suffice me to reach his gate. How can you expect me to strive to reach the Simurgh since I have lived in the earthly paradise? I have no wish except to dwell there again. Nothing else has any meaning for me.'

The Hoopoe replied: 'You are straying from the true Way. The palace of this King is far better than your paradise. You cannot do better than to strive to reach it. It is the habitation of the soul, it is eternity, it is the object of our real desires, the dwelling of the heart, the seat of truth. The Most High is a vast ocean; the paradise of earthly bliss is only a little drop; all that is not this ocean is distraction. When you can have the ocean why will you seek a drop of evening dew? Shall he who shares the secrets of the sun idle with a speck of dust? Is he who has all, concerned with the part? Is the soul concerned with members of the body? If you would be perfect seek the whole, choose the whole, be whole.'

THE MASTER AND THE PUPIL

A pupil asked his Master: 'Why was Adam obliged to leave paradise?' The Master replied: 'When Adam, the noblest of creatures, entered paradise he heard a resounding voice from the invisible world: "O you who are attached to the earthly paradise by a hundred bonds, know that whoever in the two worlds is identified with that which comes between him and me, I deprive of all that exists visibly, so that he may become attached only to me, his true friend." To a lover, a hundred thousand lives are nothing without the beloved. He who has lived for something other than Him, were it Adam himself, has been driven out. The dwellers in Paradise know that the first thing they must give up is their heart.'

6

THE DUCK

Timidly the Duck came out of the water and went up to the assembly, dressed in his finest robe. 'No one has ever spoken to a creature prettier or purer than I,' he said. 'Every hour I perform the customary ablutions, and then spread upon the water the carpet of prayer. What bird can live and move in the water as I do? In this I have a marvellous power. Among birds I am a penitent of clear sight, of clean garments; and I live in a pure element. Nothing is more profitable to me than water, for in it I find my food and have my dwelling. If troubles vex me I wash them away in water. Clear water feeds the stream wherein I live, I love not the dry earth. So, since my concern is only with water, why should I leave it? All that lives, lives by water. How shall I be able to cross the valleys and fly to the Simurgh? How can one such as I, contented with the surface of the water, have any longing to see the Simurgh?'

The Hoopoe said: 'O you whose delight is in the water which occupies your whole life! Indolently you drowse there—but a wave comes and you are swept away. Water is good only for those who have a fair countenance and a clean face. If you are such, it is well! But how long will you stay clean and pure as the water?'

STORY OF THE PIOUS MAN

Someone asked a saintly fool: 'What are the two worlds which always occupy our thoughts?' He replied: 'Both the upper and the lower worlds are as a drop of water, which is and which is not. It was a drop of water that manifested itself in the beginning, and then it assumed many lovely forms. All appearances are as water. Nothing is harder than iron, yet it knows that water is its origin. But all that has water for a basis, even iron, has no more reality than a dream. Water is nothing stable.'

7

THE PARTRIDGE

The Partridge next approached, graceful yet self-satisfied. Shyly she rises from her treasure of pearls in her garment of the dawn. With blood-rimmed eyes and red beak she flies with lightly-turning head, carrying her belt and sword.

She said: 'I like to wander among ruins for I love precious stones. They have lighted a fire in my heart and this satisfies me. When I burn with desire for them the pebbles I have swallowed become as if tinged with blood. But often I find myself between stones and fire, inactive and perplexed. O my friends, see how I live! Is it possible to awaken one who sleeps on stones and swallows gravel?

'My heart is wounded by a hundred sorrows because my love for precious stones has bound me to the mountain. Love for other things is transitory; the kingdom of the jewels is eternal, they are the essence of the everlasting mountain. I know the mountains and the precious stones. With my belt and my sword I am always seeking the diamond, and I have yet to discover a substance of a loftier

nature than precious stones—even the pearl is not as beautiful. Also, the way to the Simurgh is difficult, and my feet
are attached to the stones as if they were stuck in clay. How
can I expect to go bravely into the presence of the mighty
Simurgh, my hand on my head, my feet in the mud? Either
I will die or I will discover precious stones. My nobility is
evident, and he who does not share in my aim is not worth
considering.'

The Hoopoe said: 'O you who have colours of all the
stones, you limp a little and give lame excuses. Your heart's
blood stains your claws and beak, and your search demeans
you. What are jewels but coloured stones, yet the love of
them hardens your heart. Without their colours they would
be just ordinary little pebbles. He who possesses the perfume
does not seek the colour; he who has the essence will not
forsake it for the glitter of outward form. Seek the true
jewel of sound quality and no longer be content with a
stone.'

THE RING OF SOLOMON

No stone was ever so renowned as the stone in the Ring of
Solomon, yet it was quite a simple stone weighing no more
than half a dang. But when Solomon made a seal of it, the
whole earth came under his sway. His rule was established
and his law extended to the far horizons. Though the wind
carried his will to every quarter, he possessed only a stone
of half a dang. He said: 'Since my realm and rule depend
on this stone, from henceforth no one shall have such
power.'

Although Solomon became a great king because of his
seal, it was this that delayed his progress on the spiritual
path; and he came to the Paradise of Eden five hundred
years later than the other prophets. If a stone could produce
such a state in regard to Solomon, what could it do to a being

like you, poor Partridge? Turn your heart away from common jewels. Seek the true jewel and be always in quest of the Good Jeweller.

8

THE HUMAY

Now the Humay stood before the assembly, the Giver of Shade, whose shadow bestows pomp on kings. For this he has received the name of 'Humayun', the fortunate, since of all creatures he has the most ambition. He said: 'Birds of land and sea, I am not a bird as you are. A high ambition moves me and to satisfy it I am separated from other creatures. I have subdued the dog of desire, therefore are Feridoon and Jamshid dignified. Kings are lifted up by the influence of my shadow, but beggarly-natured men do not please me. I give a bone to my dog of desire and put my spirit in surety against it. How can men turn their head away from him whose shadow creates kings? Beneath my wings everyone seeks shelter. Do I need the friendship of the lordly Simurgh when I have royalty at my disposition?'

The Hoopoe replied: 'O slave of pride! Spread no more your shadow and boast no more of yourself. At this moment, far from conferring power upon kings you are like a dog busy with a bone. God forbid that you put a Chosroes on the throne. But supposing that your shadow sets rulers on their thrones, tomorrow they will meet misfortune and be forever deprived of their royalty, while, if they had never seen your shadow, they would not have to face so terrible a reckoning on the last day.'

MAHMŪD AND THE SAGE

A pious man who was on the true path saw Sultan Mahmūd in a dream and said to him: 'O auspicious King, how are things in the Kingdom of Eternity?' The Sultan replied:

'Strike my body if you wish but leave my soul alone. Say nothing, and depart, for here one does not speak of royalty. My power was only vanity and self-pride, conceit and error. Can sovereignty exalt a handful of earth? Sovereignty belongs to God, the Master of the Universe. Now that I have seen my weaknesses and my impotence, I am ashamed of my royalty. If you wish to give me a title, give me that of "the afflicted one". God is the King of Nature, so do not call me king. Empire belongs to him; and I would be happy now to be a simple dervish on earth. Would to God he had a hundred wells to put me in so that I had not been a ruler. Rather would I have been a gleaner in the cornfields. Call Mahmūd a slave. Give my blessings to my son Masūd, and say to him: "If you would have understanding take warning from your father's state. May the wings and the feathers wither of that Humay which cast its shadow upon me!"'

9

THE HAWK MAKES AN EXCUSE

Next came the Hawk, with head erect, and the bearing of a soldier. He said: 'I who delight in the company of kings pay no regard to other creatures. I cover my eyes with a hood so that I may put my feet on the king's hand. I am perfectly trained in polite behaviour and practise abstinence like any penitent so that when I am taken before a king I can perform my duties exactly as is expected of me. Why should I see the

Simurgh, even in a dream? Why should I rush heedlessly to him? I do not feel called upon to take part in this journey. I am content with a morsel from the king's hand; his court is good enough for me. He who plays for royal favours obtains his desire; and to be agreeable to the king I have only to take flight through the boundless valleys. I have no other wish than to pass my life joyfully in this fashion—either waiting for the king or hunting at his pleasure.'

REPLY OF THE HOOPOE

The Hoopoe said: 'O you who are attached to the outward form of things and have no care for essential values, the Simurgh is a being whose royalty becomes him, because he is unique in power. No true king exercises his will foolishly. Such a one is faithful and forgiving. Though a worldly king may often be just, he can also be guilty of injustice. The nearer one is to him, the more delicate is one's position. A believer needs must offend a king, so his life is often in danger. Since a king is compared to a fire, keep away! O you who have lived near kings, take care! Listen to this: There was once a noble king who had a slave whose body was like silver. He loved him so much that he could not be parted from him for a moment. He gave him the most beautiful clothes and set him above his fellows. But the king sometimes amused himself with shooting arrows, and would place an apple on the head of his favourite and use it as a target. And when he loosed his arrow, the slave would go yellow with fear. One day, someone said to the slave: "Why is your face the colour of gold? You are the favourite, then why this mortal pallor?" He replied: "If the king were to hit me instead of the apple, he would say: 'This slave is about the most useless thing in my court'; but when his arrow hits the mark everyone attributes it to his skill. As for me, in this painful situation, I can only hope that the king will continue to shoot straight!"'

10

THE HERON

The Heron came in all haste and at once began to speak about himself. 'My charming house is near the sea among the lagoons, where none hears my song. I am so inoffensive that no one complains of me. Sad and melancholy, I stand pensively on the salt sea's verge, my heart filled with longing for the water, for if there were none what would become of me! But since I am not one of those who dwell in the sea, I am like to die, my lips parched, on its shore. Though the waters boil and the waves break at my feet, I cannot swallow a single drop; yet if the ocean should lose even a little of its water my heart would burn with vexation. For a creature such as I my passion for the sea is enough. I have not the strength to go in quest of the Simurgh, so I ask to be excused. How could one like me, who seeks only a drop of water, possibly attain union with the Simurgh?'

Said the Hoopoe: 'O ignorant of the sea, don't you know that it is full of crocodiles and other dangerous creatures? Sometimes its water is bitter, sometimes salt; sometimes it is calm, sometimes boisterous; always changing, never stable; sometimes it flows, sometimes it ebbs. Many great ones have been swallowed up in its abyss. The diver in its depths holds his breath lest he should be thrown up like a straw. The sea is an element devoid of loyalty. Do not trust it or it will end by submerging you. It is restless because of its love for its friend. Sometimes it rolls great billows, sometimes it roars. Since the sea cannot find what it desires, how will you find there a resting place for your heart! The ocean is a rill which rises in the way that leads to its friend; why then should you remain here content, and not strive to see the face of the Simurgh?'

THE SAGE AND THE OCEAN

A sage, whose habit it was to ponder over the meaning of things, went to Ocean and asked why it wore a garment of blue, since this was the colour of mourning, and why did it boil without fire?

Ocean replied to the man of contemplation: 'I am troubled because I am separated from my friend. Because of my insufficiency I am not worthy of him, so I put on a garment of blue as a sign of the remorse I feel. In my distress the beaches of my lips are dried up, and because of the fire of my love I am in a turmoil. Could I find but a single drop of the celestial water of Kausar, I should be in possession of the gate of eternal life. Lacking this drop I shall die from desire with the thousand others who perish on the way.'

II

THE OWL

The Owl came forward with a bewildered air and said: 'I have chosen for my dwelling a ruined and tumbledown house. I was born among the ruins and there I take my delight—but not in drinking wine. I know hundreds of habited places, but some are in a state of confusion and others in a state of hatred. He who wishes to live in peace must go to the ruins, as the madmen do. If I mope among them it is because of hidden treasure. The love of treasure draws me there, for it is to be found among the ruins. Also, I can conceal my anxious quest, and hope to find a treasure that is not protected by a talisman; if my foot should light on one, my heart's desire will be achieved. I well believe that love toward the Simurgh is not a fable, for it is not experienced by the heedless; but I am feeble, and am far from being firm in his love, since I love only my treasure and my ruins.'

The Hoopoe said to him: 'O you who are drunk with love of riches, suppose you do find a treasure! Ah well, you will die on this treasure, and life will have slipped away without your having attained the high aim of which at least you are aware. Love of gold is a characteristic of infidels. He who makes an idol of gold is another Tharé. Will you not, perhaps, become as one of the Samiri of the Israelites who made the golden calf? Don't you know that everyone who has been corrupted by the love of gold will on the day of resurrection have his face changed, like a false coin, to the likeness of a mouse?'

THE MISER

A sot hid a coffer of gold, and soon after, died. A year later the son saw his father in a dream, in the form of a mouse, its two eyes full of tears. It was running backwards and forwards on the place where the gold was hidden. His son asked him: 'What are you doing here?' The father replied: 'I hid some gold and have come to see if anyone has discovered it.' 'Why do you have the form of a mouse?' asked the son. The father said: 'The soul of the man who has given up everything for the love of money assumes this form. Take note of me, O my son, and profit by what you see. Renounce the love of gold!'

12

THE SPARROW

Then came the Sparrow, of feeble body and tender heart, trembling like a flame from head to foot. She said: 'I am dumbfounded and crestfallen. I don't know how to exist, and I am frail as a hair. I have no one to help me and I have not the strength of an ant. I have neither down nor feathers —nothing. How can a weakling like me make her way to the Simurgh? A sparrow could never do it. There is no lack of those in the world who seek this union, but for a being such as I it is not becoming. I do not wish to begin such a toilsome journey for something I can never reach. If I should start out for the court of the Simurgh I should be consumed on the way. So since I am not at all fitted for this enterprise I shall be content to seek here my Joseph in the well. If I find him and draw him out I shall soar with him from the fish to the moon.'

The Hoopoe replied: 'O you, who in your despondency are sometimes sad, sometimes gay, I am not deceived by these artful pleas. You are a little hypocrite. Even in your humility you show a hundred signs of vanity and pride. Not another word, sew up your lips and put your foot forward. If you burn, you will burn with the others. And don't compare yourself with Joseph!'

STORY OF JACOB

When Joseph was taken, his father Jacob lost his sight because of the tears of blood that flowed from his eyes. The name of Joseph was always on his lips. At last the Angel Gabriel went to him and said: 'If ever again you utter the word "Joseph" I will strike your name from the roll of prophets and messengers.' When Jacob received this message from God the name of Joseph was lifted from his tongue, but he did not cease to repeat it in his heart. One night he saw Joseph in a dream, and would have called to him, but remembering God's command, he beat his breast and heaved a sad sigh from his immaculate heart. Then Gabriel came: 'God says that although you have not pronounced the name "Joseph" with your tongue, you have heaved a sigh, and thus destroyed all the effect of your repentance.'

13

DISCUSSION BETWEEN THE HOOPOE AND THE BIRDS

Then all the birds, one after another, began to make foolish excuses. If I do not repeat them, pardon me, reader, for it would take too long. But how can such birds hope to entangle the Simurgh in their claws? So the Hoopoe continued her discourse:

'He who prefers the Simurgh to his own life must struggle bravely with himself. If your gizzard will not digest a single grain how shall you share in the feasting of the Simurgh? When you hesitate over a sip of wine how will you drink a large cup, O paladin? If you have not the energy for an atom how shall you find the treasure of the sun? If you can drown in a drop of water, how will you go from the depths of the sea to the heavenly heights? This is not a simple perfume; and neither is it a task for him who has not a clean face.'

When the birds had thought this over they again spoke to the Hoopoe: 'You have taken upon yourself the task of showing us the way, you, the best and most powerful of birds. But we are feeble, with neither down nor feathers, so how shall we be able at last to reach the Sublime Simurgh? If we should arrive it would be a miracle. Tell us something about this marvellous Being by means of a similitude, or, blind as we are, we shall understand nothing of the mystery. If there were some relation between this Being and ourselves it would be much easier for us to set out. But, as we see it, he may be compared to Solomon, and we to begging ants. How can an insect in the bottom of a pit mount up to the great Simurgh? Shall royalty be the portion of the beggar?'

REPLY OF THE HOOPOE

The Hoopoe said: 'O birds without aspiration! How shall love spring bountifully in a heart devoid of sensibility? Begging the question like this, which seems to gratify you, will result in nothing. He who loves sets out with open eyes towards his goal making a plaything of his life.

'When the Simurgh manifested himself outside the veil, radiant as the sun, he produced thousands of shadows on earth. When he cast his glance on these shadows there appeared birds in great numbers. The different types of birds that are seen in the world are thus only the shadow of the Simurgh. Know then, O ignorant ones, that when you understand this you will understand exactly your relation to the Simurgh. Ponder over this mystery, but do not reveal it. He who acquires this knowledge sinks into the immensity of the Simurgh; though he must not think that he is God on that account.

'If you become this of which I speak you will not be God, but you will be immersed in God. Does a man thus immersed become transubstantiated? When you understand of whom you are the shadow you will become indifferent to life or death. If the Simurgh had not wished to manifest himself he would not have cast his shadow; if he had wished to remain hidden his shadow would not have appeared in the world. All that which is produced by his shadow becomes visible. If your spirit is not fit to see the Simurgh, neither will your heart be a bright mirror, fit to reflect him. It is true that no eye is able to contemplate and marvel at his beauty, nor is it capable of understanding; one cannot feel towards the Simurgh as one feels towards the beauty of this world. But by his abounding grace he has given us a mirror to reflect himself, and this mirror is the heart. Look into your heart and there you will see his image.'

THE CHARMING KING

There was once a king of incomparable charm and beauty. The dawn was a flash of lightning from his countenance, the Angel Gabriel an emanation of his fragrance and the kingdom of beauty was the Koran of his secrets. The whole world resounded with his fame, and his love was felt by every creature. When he rode through the city he covered his face with a crimson veil; but those who looked even at the veil lost their heads, and those who uttered his name at once cut out their tongues. Thousands died for love of him; others gave their lives believing it better to die at once than to live a hundred long lives away from him. An astonishing thing! They could neither endure his presence for long nor could they exist without him. However, to those who could endure it he showed himself; those who could not had to be content to hear his voice. In consequence, the king ordered a mirror to be made so that his face could be seen indirectly. The mirror was put up in his palace, and he went and looked in it, so that all could see his reflection.

So it is with you. If you cherish the beauty of your friend, understand that your heart is the mirror, see in it your king in the mansion of his glory. All appearances are nothing but the mysterious shadow of the Simurgh. If he had revealed his beauty to you, you would have recognized it in his shadow. Whether there were thirty birds, 'Si-murgh', or forty, you would only see his shadow. The Simurgh is not distinct from his shadow, to hold the contrary is to err; the one and the other exist together. Seek reunion; or better, leave the shadow and you will discover the Secret. With good fortune you will see the Sun in the shadow; but if you lose yourself in the shadow, how will you achieve union with the Simurgh?

MAHMŪD AND AYĀZ

Ayāz was afflicted with the evil eye, and had to leave the court of the Sultan Mahmūd. In despair he fell into a state of despondency and lay on his bed and wept. When Mahmūd heard about it he said to one of his attendants: 'Go to Ayāz and say, "I know that you are sad, but I also am in the same state. Though my body is far from you my spirit is near. O you who love me, I am not absent from you for a moment. The evil eye has indeed done ill in afflicting one so charming."' He added to his attendant: 'Go at once, go like fire, go as the rushing water, go as the lightning before the thunder!'

The attendant set off like the wind and in no time reached Ayāz. But he found the Sultan already there, sitting before his slave. And trembling, he said to himself: 'What a misfortune to have to serve a king; no doubt my blood will be shed today.' Then he said to the Sultan: 'I assure you that I haven't stopped for a moment, sitting or standing; how then has the King got here before me? Does the King believe me? If I have been negligent in any way I acknowledge my fault.'

'You are not Mahrām,' said Mahmūd, 'how then should you be able to travel as I have? I came by a secret way. When I asked for news of Ayāz my spirit was already with him.'

14

THE HOOPOE TELLS THEM ABOUT THE PROPOSED JOURNEY

When she had finished her discourse the birds began to understand something of the ancient mysteries, and the relation between themselves and the Simurgh. But though they were seized with a desire to make the journey they flinched from setting out, for doubts still disturbed their minds, so they said to the Hoopoe: 'Do you wish us to give up our tranquil lives at once? We feeble birds by ourselves cannot expect to find the way to that sublime abode where the Simurgh has his being.'

The Hoopoe replied: 'I speak to you as your guide. He who loves does not think about his own life; to love truly a man must forget about himself, be he ascetic or libertine. If your desires do not accord with your spirit, sacrifice them, and you will come to the end of your journey. If the body of desire obstructs the way, reject it; then fix your eyes in front and contemplate. An ignorant person will ask, "What connection is there between belief or unbelief, and love?" But I say, "Do lovers regard their lives? The lover sets fire to all hope of harvest, he puts the blade to his neck, he pierces his body. With love comes sorrow and the heart's blood. Love loves the difficult things."

'O Cup-bearer! Fill my cup with the blood of my heart and if there be no more, give me the lees. Love is a cruel pain that devours everything. Sometimes it tears the veil from the soul, sometimes it draws it together. An atom of love is preferable to all that exists between the horizons, an atom of its pain better than the happy love of all lovers. Love is the very marrow of beings; but there can be no real love without real suffering. Whoever is grounded firm in love renounces faith, religion, and unbelief. Love will open the door of spiritual poverty and poverty will show you the way of unbelief. When there remains neither unbelief nor religion, your body and your soul will disappear; you will then be worthy of the mysteries—if you would fathom them, this is the only way.

'Go forward then, without fear. Forsake childish things and, above all, take courage; for a hundred vicissitudes will come upon you unawares.'

STORY OF SHAIKH SAN'AN

The Shaikh San'an was a saintly man in his day, and had perfected himself to a high degree. For fifty years he had remained in his retreat with four hundred disciples, who worked on themselves day and night. He had great knowledge, and benefited by outer and inner revelation. Much of his life had been spent in making pilgrimages to Mecca. His prayers and fasts were without number and he omitted none of the practices of the Sunnites. He could work miracles, and his breath healed the sick and depressed.

One night he dreamed that he went from Mecca to Greece and there worshipped an idol; and waking grief-stricken from this oppressive dream he said to his disciples: 'I must set out at once for Greece to see if I can discover the meaning of this dream.'

With his four hundred disciples he left the Ka'aba and in time arrived in Greece. They travelled from end to end of that country, and one day by chance came to where a young girl was sitting on a balcony. This girl was a Christian, and the expression of her face showed that she possessed the faculty of pondering on the things of God. Her beauty was like the sun in splendour, and her dignity as the Signs of the Zodiac. From jealousy of her radiance the morning star loitered above her house. Who caught his heart in her hair put on the belt of a Christian; whose desire lighted on the ruby of her lips lost his head. The morn took on a darker tint because of her black hair, the land of Greece wrinkled up because of the beauty of her freckles. Her two eyes were a lure for lovers; her arched brows formed tender sickles over twin moons. When power lighted the pupils of her eyes a hundred hearts became her prey. Her face sparkled like a living flame, and the moist rubies of her lips could make a whole world thirst. Her languorous lashes were a hundred daggers, and her mouth was so small that even words could not pass. Her waist, slender as a hair, was squeezed through her zunnar; and the silver dimple of her chin was as vivifying as the discourses of Jesus.'

When she lifted a corner of her veil the heart of the shaikh took fire; and a single hair bound his loins with a hundred zunnars. He could not take his eyes from this young Christian, and such was his love that his will slipped from his hands. Unbelief from her hair strewed itself on his faith. He cried out: 'Oh, how terrible is this love that I have for her. When religion leaves you, of what good is the heart!'

When his companions understood what had happened, and saw the state he was in, they held their heads in their hands. Some began to reason with him, but he refused to listen. He could only stand day and night, his eyes fixed on the balcony and his mouth open. The stars that glowed like lamps borrowed heat from this holy man whose heart was on fire. His love grew until he was beside himself. 'O Lord,' he prayed, 'in my life I have fasted and suffered, but never have I suffered like this; I am in torment. The night is as long and as black as her hair. Where is the lamp of Heaven? Have my sighs extinguished it or has it hidden itself from jealousy? Where is my good fortune? Why does it not help me to get the love of this girl? Where is my reason to make use of my knowledge? Where is my hand to put dust on my head? Where is my foot to walk to my beloved, and my eye to see her face? Where is my beloved to give me her heart? What is this love, this grief, this pain?'

The friends of the shaikh came again to him. One said: 'O worthy shaikh, lift yourself up and drive away this temptation. Take hold of yourself and perform the ordained ablutions.' He replied: 'Do you not know that this night I have made a hundred ablutions, and with my heart's blood?' Another said: 'Where is your chaplet? How can you pray without it?' He replied: 'I have thrown away my chaplet so that I may girdle myself with a Christian zunnar.' Another said: 'O saintly old man, if you have sinned repent without delay.' 'I repent now,' he replied, 'of having followed the true law, and I only wish to give up that absurdity.' Another said: 'Leave this place and go and worship God.' He replied: 'If my idol were here it would become me to bow down before her.' Another said: 'Then, you will not even try to repent! Are you no longer a follower of Islam?' The shaikh replied: 'No one repents more than I that I was not in love until now.' Another said: 'The infernal regions are waiting for you if you continue on this path; but watch yourself, and you will avoid them.' He replied: 'If hell is there it is only from my sighs, which would feed seven hells.'

Seeing that their words produced no effect on the shaikh, although they pleaded with him all night, his friends went away. Meanwhile the Turk of the Morning, with sabre and golden buckler, cut off the head of Black Night, so that the world of illusion was bathed in the radiance of the Sun. The shaikh, plaything of his love, wandered with the dogs, and for a month sat in the street hoping to see her face. The dust was his bed and her doorstep his pillow.

Then the beautiful Christian, seeing that he was hopelessly in love, veiled herself, and went out and said to him: 'O shaikh, how is it that you, an ascetic, are so drunk with the wine of polytheism, and sit in a Christian street in such a state? If you adore me like this you will go mad.' The shaikh replied: 'It is because you have stolen my heart. Either give it back or accept my love. If you wish I will lay down my life for you, but you may restore that life by a touch of your lips. Because of you my heart is on fire. I have shed tears like rain and my eyes have lost their sight. Where my heart was there is only blood. If I were united to you my life would be restored. You are the sun, I the shadow. I am a lost man, but if you will incline to me I will take under my wing the seven cupolas of the world. Do not leave me, I implore you!'

'O you old driveller!' she said, 'aren't you ashamed to
use camphor for your winding sheet? You should blush for
suggesting intimacy with me with your cold breath! You
had better wrap yourself in a shroud than spend your time
on me. You cannot inspire love. Go away!'

The shaikh replied: 'Say what you will, I still love you.
What does it matter whether one is young or old, love
affects all hearts.'

She said: 'Very well, if you are not to be denied, listen to
me. You must wash your hands of Islam; for love which is
not identified with its beloved is only colour and perfume.'

He said: 'I will do all that you wish. I will undertake all
that you command, you, whose body is like silver. I am
your slave. Put a lock of your hair on my neck to remind
me of my slavery.'

'If you are a man of action,' said the young Christian, 'you
must do four things: prostrate yourself before the idols, burn
the Koran, drink wine, and shut your eyes to your religion.'

He said: 'I will drink wine to your beauty but the other
three things I cannot do.' 'Very well,' she said, 'come and
drink wine with me, then you will soon accept the other
conditions.'

She led him to a temple of magicians, where he saw a
very strange gathering. They sat down to a banquet at which
the hostess was distinguished by her beauty. His beloved
handed him a cup of wine, and when he took it and looked
at the smiling rubies of her lips, like two lids of a casket,
the fire blazed in his heart and a stream of blood rushed to
his eyes. He tried to recall the sacred books he had read and
written on religion, and the Koran that he knew so well;
but when the wine passed from the cup into his stomach he
forgot them all; his spiritual knowledge was washed away.
He lost his free will and let slip his heart from his hand.
When he tried to put his hand on her neck, she said: 'You
only pretend to love. You do not understand the mystery

of love. If you are sure of your love you may find the way to my curled locks. Lose yourself in unbelief by the way of my tangled ringlets; follow the locks of my hair, and you may put your hand on my neck. But if you do not wish to follow my way, get up and go; and take the cloak and staff of a faquir.'

At this, the amorous shaikh was crestfallen; and now he yielded without more ado to his destiny. The wine he had drunk made his head as uncertain as a compass. The wine was old and his love was young. How could he have been otherwise than drunk and in love?

'O Splendour of the Moon,' he said, 'tell me what you wish. If I was not an idolater before I lost my wits, now that I am drunk I will burn the Koran before the idol.'

The young beauty said: 'You are now really my man. You are worthy of me. Till now you were uncooked in love, but having acquired experience you are roasted. Good!'

When the Christians heard that the shaikh had embraced their faith they carried him, still drunk, into the church and told him to girdle himself with a zunnar. He did this and threw his dervish mantle into the fire, forsook the Faith, and delivered himself up to the practices of the Christian religion.

He said to the girl: 'O charming lady, no one has ever done as much for a woman as I have done. I have worshipped your idols, I have drunk wine, and I have given up the true Faith. All this I have done for love of you, and that I may have you.'

Again she said to him: 'Old driveller, slave of love, how can a woman such as I be united to a faquir? I need silver and gold, and since you have none, take your head and go.'

The shaikh said: 'O lovely woman, your body is a cypress and your breasts are silver. If you repulse me you will drive me to despair. The thought of possessing you has thrown me into a turmoil. On account of you my friends have become my enemies. As you are, so are they; what shall I do? O my beloved, I had rather be in hell with you than in paradise without you.'

At last she relented, and the shaikh became her man, and she too began to feel the flame of love. But to try him further she said: 'Now, for my dowry, O imperfect man, go and look after my herd of pigs for the space of a year, and then we shall pass our lives together in joy or sadness!' Without a protest, this shaikh of the Ka'aba, this saint, resigned himself to becoming a hog-ward.

In the nature of each of us there are a hundred pigs. O you, who are non-entities, you are thinking only of the danger that the shaikh was in! The danger is to be found in each one of us, and it raises its head from the moment we start out on the path of self-knowledge. If you do not know your own pigs then you do not know the Path. But if you do set out you will meet a thousand pigs—a thousand idols. Drive away these pigs, burn these idols on the plain of love; or else be like the shaikh, dishonoured by love.

Well, then, when the news spread that the shaikh had become a Christian, his companions were in great distress and all but one went away, who said to him: 'Tell us the secret of this matter so that we may become Christians with you. We do not wish you to remain an apostate alone, so we will take the Christian zunnar. If you do not agree we shall return to the Ka'aba and spend our time in prayer in order not to see that which we see now.'

The shaikh said: 'My soul is full of sadness. Go where your wishes carry you. As for me, the church is my place, and the young Christian my destiny. Do you know why you are free? It is because you are not in my position. If you were, I should have a companion in my unhappy love. Return then, dear friend, to the Ka'aba, for no one can share my present state. If they should ask about me say: "His eyes are full of blood, his mouth full of poison; he remains in the jaws of the dragons of violence. No infidel would consent to do what this proud Musulmān has done by the effect of destiny. A young Christian has caught his neck in a noose of her hair." If they reproach me, say that many fall by the way on this road which has neither beginning nor end, but some by chance will be safe from descent and danger.' With this he turned his face from his friend and went back to the herd.

His followers, who had been watching from a distance, wept bitterly. Finally, they journeyed back to the Ka'aba, and ashamed and bewildered hid themselves in a corner.

Now in the Ka'aba there was a friend of the shaikh who was a seer, and who was on the true path. No one knew the shaikh better than he, though he had not accompanied him to Greece. When this man asked for news the disciples related all that had happened to the shaikh, and they asked what ugly branch of a tree had pierced his breast, and whether this had happened by the will of fate. They said that a young infidel had bound him with a single hair and barred him from the hundred ways of Islam. 'He dallies with her ringlets and freckles, and has burnt his khirka. He has forsaken his religion and now girdled with a zunnar he looks after a herd of pigs. But though he has staked his very soul we feel there is still hope.'

Hearing this, the disciple's face turned the colour of gold, and he began to lament bitterly. Then he said: 'Companions in misfortune, in religion there is neither man nor woman. When an unfortunate friend needs help it sometimes happens that only a single person in a thousand can be of use.' He then reproached them for leaving the shaikh and said that they should even have become Christians for his sake. He added: 'A friend must remain a friend. It is in misfortune that you discover on whom you can rely; for in good fortune you will have a thousand friends. Now that the shaikh has fallen into the crocodile's jaws everyone stays away from him in order to keep their reputation. If you shun him because of this strange happening you will have been tried and found wanting.'

'We offered to stay with him,' they said, 'and even agreed to become idolaters. But he is an experienced and learned man, and we trust him, so when he told us to go, we returned here.'

The faithful disciple replied: 'If you really wish to act you must knock on the door of God; then, by prayer, you will be admitted to his presence. You should have been pleading with God for your shaikh, each reciting a different prayer; and God, seeing your bewildered state, would have given him back to you. Why have you refrained from knocking at the door of God?'

At this they were ashamed to raise their heads. But he said: 'This is no time for regrets. Let us go now to the court of God. Let us lie in the dust, and cover ourselves with the garment of supplication that we may recover our leader!'

The disciples at once set out for Greece, and having arrived there remained near the shaikh. For forty days and forty nights they prayed. During these forty days and forty nights they neither ate nor slept; they tasted neither bread nor water. At last the power of the prayers of these sincere men made itself felt in Heaven. Angels and archangels and all the Saints robed in green on the heights and in the valleys, now arrayed themselves in the garments of mourning. The arrow of prayer had reached its mark. When morning came, a musk-laden zephyr blew softly upon the faithful disciple at prayer in his cell, and the world was unveiled to his spirit. He saw the Prophet Muhammad approaching, radiant as the morn, two locks of hair falling upon his breast; the shadow of God was the sun of his countenance, the desire of a hundred worlds was attached to each of his hairs. His gracious smile drew all men to him. The disciple rose up and said: 'O messenger of God, the guide of all creatures, help me! Our shaikh has strayed. Show him the way, I implore you in the name of the Most High!'

Muhammad said: 'O you who see things with the inner eye, because of your efforts your pure desires shall be gratified. Between the shaikh and God there has been for a long time a black speck; but I have poured out the dew of supplication and have scattered it on the dust of his existence. He has repented and his sin is wiped away. The faults of a hundred worlds can disappear in the vapour of a moment of repentance. When the ocean of good-will is moved its waves wash out the sins of men and women.'

The disciple uttered a cry that moved all heaven. He ran and told his companions the good news, then weeping for joy hastened to where the shaikh was keeping the pigs. But the shaikh was as a fire, as one illumined. He had cast off the Christian belt, thrown away the girdle, torn the bonnet of drunkenness from his head and renounced Christianity. He saw himself as he was and shedding tears of remorse lifted his hands to heaven; all that he had forsaken—the Koran, the mysteries and prophecies, came back to him, and he was delivered from his misery and folly. They said to him: 'Now is the hour of gratitude and thankfulness. The Prophet has interceded for you. Thanks be to God that he has lifted you out of an ocean of pitch and placed your foot on the way of the Sun.'

The shaikh thereupon resumed his khirka, performed his ablutions, and set out for the Hejaz.

While this was happening the Christian girl saw in a dream the sun descending to her, and heard these words: 'Follow your shaikh, embrace his faith, be his dust. You who are soiled, be pure as he is now. You led him in your way, enter now in his.'

She woke; a light broke on her spirit, and she longed to set out on her quest. Her hand seized her heart, and her heart fell from her hand. But when she realized that she was

alone, and had no idea of the way, her joy was changed to
weeping and she ran out to throw dust on her head. Then
she started out in pursuit of the shaikh and his disciples; but
growing weary and distraught, covered with sweat, she
threw herself on the ground and cried out: 'May God the
Creator forgive me! I am a woman, disgusted with life. Do
not strike me down, for I struck you in ignorance and
through ignorance committed many faults. Forget the ill I
have done. I accept the true Faith.'

An inner voice apprised the shaikh of this. He stopped,
and said: 'That young girl is no longer an infidel. Light has
come to her and she has entered our Way. Let us go back.
One can now be intimately bound to one's idol without sin.'

But his companions said: 'Now what is the use of all
your repentance and remorse! Are you going back to your
love?' He told them of the voice he had heard, and reminded
them that he had renounced his former ways. So they went
back until they came to where the girl lay. Her face had
gone the colour of yellow gold, her feet were bare, her dress
torn. As the shaikh bent down to her she swooned away.
When she came to herself her tears fell like dew from roses,
and she said: 'I am consumed with shame because of you.
Lift the veil of the secret and instruct me in Islam so that I
may walk in the Way.'

When this fair idol was at last numbered among the faithful, the companions shed tears of joy. But her heart was
impatient to be delivered from sorrow. 'O shaikh,' she said,
'my strength is gone. I wish to leave this dusty deafening
world. Farewell, Shaikh San'an. I confess my faults.
Pardon me, and let me go.'

So this moon of beauty who had had no more than half
a life, shook it from her hand. The sun hid itself behind the
clouds while her sweet soul separated itself from her body.
She, a drop in the ocean of illusion, had returned to the true
ocean.

We all leave as the wind; she is gone and we also shall go. Such things often happen in the way of love. There is despair and mercy, illusion and security. Though the body of desire cannot understand the secrets, adversity cannot knock away the polo ball of good fortune. One must hear with the ear of the mind and the heart, not with that of the body. The struggle of the spirit with the body of desire is unending. Lament! For there is cause to mourn.

15

THE BIRDS DISCUSS THE PROPOSED JOURNEY TO THE SIMURGH

When they had pondered over the story of Shaikh San'an, the birds decided to give up all their former way of life. The thought of the Simurgh lifted them out of their apathy; love for him alone filled their hearts, and they began to consider how to start on the journey. They said: 'First, we must have a guide to tie and untie the knots. We need a leader who will tell us what to do, one who can save us from this deep sea. We will obey him from our hearts and do what he says, be it pleasant or unpleasant, so that our ball will fall on the mallet of the Caucasus. Then the atom will be united to the majestic sun; and the shadow of the Simurgh will fall on us. Now, let us draw lots for a leader. He on whom the lot falls shall be our guide; he shall be great among the small.'

Then began a commotion, everyone talking at once, but when everything was ready, the twittering and chattering died down and the birds fell silent. The drawing was conducted with due ceremony, and eventually the lot fell on the spirited Hoopoe. All with one accord agreed and promised to obey her even at the risk of their lives, and to spare neither soul nor body. The Hoopoe came forward and a crown was placed on her head.

At the setting-out place, so great was the number of birds who flocked there that they hid the moon and the fish; but when they saw the entrance to the first valley, they flew up to the clouds in fright. Then, with much fluttering of wings and feathers and mutual encouragement, their eagerness to renounce everything revived. But the task before them was heavy and the way was long. Silence brooded over the road which stretched before them and a bird asked the Hoopoe why it was so deserted. 'Because of the awe that the King inspires, to whose dwelling it leads' she answered.

ANECDOTE OF BĀYĀZID BISTĀMI

One night when the Shaikh Bāyāzid went out from the town he noticed that a profound silence lay over the plain. The moon lighted the world making the night as bright as day. The stars clustered according to their sympathies, and each constellation had its special function. The shaikh walked on without seeing any movement or a single soul. His heart was stirred and he said: 'Lord, a piercing sadness moves me. Why is it that a court so sublime is without eager worshippers?' 'Be not amazed,' an inner voice answered, 'the King does not admit everyone to his court. His dignity does not suffer him to receive tramps at his door. When the sanctuary of our splendour sheds its effulgence it disdains the sleepy and the heedless. You are one of a thousand who crave admission and you must wait patiently.'

16

THE BIRDS SET OUT

Fear and apprehension drew plaintive cries from the birds as they faced a road without end, where the strong wind of detachment from earthly things split the vault of heaven. In their anxiety they crowded together and asked the Hoopoe for advice. They said: 'We do not know how we should present ourselves to the King with due reverence. But you have been in the presence of Solomon, and know the usages of etiquette. Also you have ascended and descended this road, and many times flown round the earth. You are our Imām, to bind and to loose. We ask you now to go up into the minabar and instruct us. Tell us about the road and about the King's court and the ceremonies there, for we do not wish to behave foolishly. Also, all kinds of difficulties arise in our minds, and for this journey one needs to be free from disquiet. We have many questions to ask, and we wish you to resolve our misgivings, otherwise we shall not see clearly on this long road.'

The Hoopoe then set the crown on her head, sat on her throne and disposed herself to speak to them. When the army of birds was ranged in front of her in ranks, the Nightingale and the Turtle-dove went up and as two readers with the same voice together gave forth a melody so sweet that all who heard were lifted out of themselves. Then one after another, a number of birds went up to her to speak about their difficulties and to make excuses.

17

SPEECH OF THE FIRST BIRD

The first bird said to the Hoopoe: 'O you who have been made our leader, tell us what makes you stand out from us. Since you seem to be as us, and we as you, in what lies the difference? What sins of the body or of the soul have we committed that we are ignorant while you have understanding?'

The Hoopoe replied: 'Know, O bird, that Solomon once saw me by chance; and that my good fortune was not the result of gold or silver, but of this lucky meeting. How can a creature profit from obedience alone? Iblis himself obeys. Nevertheless, if anyone counsels the rejection of obedience then malediction shall be on him for ever. Practise obedience and you will win a glance from the true Solomon.'

MAHMŪD AND THE FISHERMAN

Sultan Mahmūd was once separated from his army, and all alone galloped away like the wind. By and by he saw a small boy sitting on the bank of a river into which he had cast his net. The Sultan went up to him and noticing that he was dejected and depressed said: 'Dear child, what makes you so sad? Never have I seen anyone so cast down.' 'O Illustrious Prince,' he replied, 'there are seven of us; we have no father, and our mother is very poor. Each day I come and try to catch fish for supper. Only when I succeed in landing some do we have an evening meal.'

'Would you like me to have a try?' asked the Sultan. The boy consenting, the Sultan cast the net, which, sharing in his good fortune quickly took a hundred fish. At this, the boy said to himself, 'My fortune is astonishing. What luck that all these fish have tumbled into my net.' But the Sultan said: 'Don't deceive yourself, my child. I am the cause of your good luck. The Sultan has caught these fish for you.' So saying, he mounted his horse. The boy asked him to take his share, but the Sultan refused, saying that he would take the next day's catch. 'Tomorrow, you shall fish for me,' he said. He then returned to his palace. Next day he sent one of his officers for the boy. When they arrived he made the boy sit on the throne beside him. 'Sire,' said one of his courtiers, 'this boy is a beggar!' 'Never mind,' replied the Sultan, 'he is now my companion. Seeing that we have formed a partnership I cannot send him away.' So the Sultan treated him as an equal. At last someone asked the boy, 'How has it come about that you are so honoured?' The boy replied: 'Joy has come, and sorrow is past, because I met with a fortunate monarch.'

MAHMŪD AND THE WOODCUTTER

Another time when Sultan Mahmūd was riding alone he met an old woodcutter leading his donkey loaded with brambles. At that moment the donkey stumbled, and as he fell the thorns skinned the old man's head. The Sultan seeing the brambles on the ground, the donkey upside down, and the man rubbing his head, asked: 'O unlucky man, do you need a friend?' 'Indeed I do,' replied the woodcutter. 'Good cavalier, if you will help me I shall reap the benefit and you will come to no harm. Your looks are a good omen for me. It is well known that one meets with good-will from those who have a pleasing countenance.' So the kind-hearted Sultan got off his horse, and having pulled the donkey to its feet, lifted up the faggot of thorns and fastened it on its back. Then he rode off to rejoin his army. He said to the soldiers: 'An old woodcutter is coming along with a donkey loaded with brambles. Bar the way so that he will have to pass in front of me.' When the woodcutter came up to the soldiers he said to himself, 'How shall I get through with this feeble beast?' So he went by another way, but catching sight of the royal parasol in the distance began to tremble, for the road he was compelled to take would bring him face to face with the Sultan. As he got nearer he was overcome with confusion for under the parasol he saw a familiar face. 'O God,' he said, 'what a state I'm in! Today I have had Mahmūd for my porter.'

When he came up, Mahmūd said to him: 'My poor friend, what do you do for a living?' The woodcutter replied, 'You know already. Be honest. You don't recognize me? I am a poor old man, a woodcutter by trade; day and night I gather brambles in the desert and sell them, yet my donkey dies of hunger. If you wish me well give me some bread.' 'You poor man,' said the Sultan, 'how much do you want for your faggot?' The woodcutter replied: 'Since you do not wish to take it for nothing and I do not wish to sell it, give me a purse of gold.' At this the soldiers cried out: 'Hold your tongue, fool! Your faggot is not worth a handful of barley. You should give it for nothing.' The old man said: 'That is all very well, but its value has changed. When a lucky man like the Sultan puts his hands to my bundle of thorns they become bunches of roses. If he wishes to buy them he must pay a dinar at the very least for he has raised the value of my thorns a hundred times by touching them.'

18

SPEECH OF THE SECOND BIRD

Another bird came up to the Hoopoe and said: 'O protectress of the army of Solomon! I have not the strength to undertake this journey. I am too weak to cross the valleys. The road is so difficult that I shall lie down and die at the first stage. There are volcanoes in the way. Also, it is not expedient for everyone to engage in such an enterprise. Thousands of heads have rolled like the balls in polo, for many have perished who went in quest of the Simurgh. On such a road, where many sincere creatures have hidden their heads in fear, what shall become of me, who am only dust?'

The Hoopoe replied: 'O you of the doleful countenance! Why is your heart so oppressed? Since you are of so little value in the world it is all the same whether you be young and valiant or old and feeble. The world is truly ordure; creatures perish there at every door. Thousands turn yellow as silk, and perish in the midst of tears and affliction. It is better to lose your life in the quest than to languish miserably. If we should not succeed, but die of grief, ah well, so much the worse, but, since errors are numerous in this world, we may at least avoid acquiring new ones. Thousands of creatures are craftily occupied in the pursuit of the dead body of the world; so, if you give yourself up to this commerce, above all with guile, will you be able to make your heart an ocean of love? Some say that the wish for spiritual things is presumption, and that no mere upstart can attain them. But isn't it better to sacrifice one's life in pursuit of this desire than to be identified with a business? I have seen everything and done everything, and nothing will shake my resolve. For a long time I have had to do with men and have seen how few there be who are truly unattached to riches. So long as we do not die to ourselves, and so long as we are identified with someone or something, we shall never be free. The spiritual way is not for those wrapped up in exterior life. Set your foot in this Way if you are a man who can act, and do not indulge in feminine shifts. Know surely, that even if this quest were impious, it would still be necessary to undertake it. Certainly, it is not easy; the fruit is without leaves on the tree of love. Tell him who has leaves to renounce them.

'When love possesses a man it lifts his heart, it plunges him in blood, it throws him prostrate outside the curtain, it gives him no rest for a single instant; it kills him yet still demands the price of blood. He drinks the water of tears and eats bread leavened with mourning; but be he more feeble than an ant, love will lend him strength.'

ANECDOTE OF A CONTEMPLATIVE

A madman, a fool of God, went naked when other men went clothed. He said: 'O God, give me a beautiful garment, then I shall be content as other men.' A voice from the unseen world answered him: 'I have given you a warm sun, sit down and revel in it.' The madman said: 'Why punish

me? Haven't you a better garment than the sun?' The voice
said: 'Wait patiently for ten days, and without more ado I
will give you another garment.' The sun scorched him for
eight days; then a poor man came along and gave him a
garment which had a thousand patches. The fool said to
God: 'O you who have knowledge of hidden things, why
have you given me this patched-up garment? Have you
burnt all your garments and had to patch up this old one?
You have sewn together a thousand garments. From whom
have you learned this art?'

It is not easy to have dealings at the Court of God. A man
must become as the dust of the road which leads there. After
a long struggle he thinks he has reached the goal only to
discover that it is still to be attained.

STORY OF RĀBI'AH

Rābi'ah, although a woman, was the crown of men. She
once spent eight years making a pilgrimage to the Ka'aba
by measuring her length on the ground. When at last she
reached the door of the sacred temple she thought: 'Now at
last, have I performed my task.' On the consecrated day,
when she was to go in to the Ka'aba, her women deserted
her. So Rābi'ah retraced her steps and said: 'O God, possessor of glory, for eight years I have measured the way with
the length of my body, and now, when the longed-for day
has come in answer to my prayers, you put thorns in my
way!'

To understand the importance of such an incident it is
necessary to discover a lover of God like Rābi'ah. So long
as you float on the deep ocean of the world its waves will
receive and repel you, turn by turn. At times you will be
admitted into the Ka'aba, sometimes you will sigh in a
pagoda. If you succeed in withdrawing from the attachments of the world you will enjoy felicity; but if you

remain attached your head will turn like the grindstone of
a mill. Not for a moment will you be tranquil; you will be
upset by a single fly.

THE FOOL OF GOD

It was the custom of a poor man in love with God to stand
in a certain place; and one day a king of Egypt who had
often passed him with his courtiers, stopped, and said: 'I
see in you a certain quality of tranquillity and relaxation.'
The fool replied: 'How should I be tranquil, seeing that I
am delivered up to the flies and the fleas? All day the flies
torment me, and at night the fleas won't let me sleep. One
tiny fly which entered the ear of Nimrod troubled the brain
of that idiot for centuries. Perhaps I am the Nimrod of these
times for I have had my share of my friends, the flies and the
fleas.'

19

SPEECH OF THE THIRD BIRD

The third bird said to the Hoopoe: 'I am full of faults, so
how shall I set out on the road? Can a dirty fly be worthy
of the Simurgh of the Caucasus? How can a sinner who
turns away from the true path approach the King?'

The Hoopoe said: 'O despondent bird, do not be so
hopeless, ask for grace and favour. If you so lightly throw
away the shield your task truly will be difficult.'

ANECDOTE OF A CRIMINAL

A man guilty of many sins repented bitterly and returned to
the right path. But in time, his desire for the things of the
world returned stronger than ever, and he again surrendered
himself to evil thoughts and acts. Then sorrow wrung his
heart and reduced him to a miserable state. Again he wished

to change his attitude, but had not the strength to do so. Day and night as a grain of wheat in a hot pan, his heart could not keep still, and his tears watered the dust. One morning, a mysterious voice spoke to him: 'Listen to the Lord of the World. When you repented the first time I accepted your penitence. Though I could have punished you I did not do so. A second time when you fell into sin I gave you a respite, and now even in my anger I have not caused you to die. And today, O fool, you acknowledge your perfidy and wish to return to me a third time. Return then, to the Way. I open my door to you and wait. When you have truly changed your attitude your sins will be forgiven.'

THE ANGEL GABRIEL AND THE GOOD INTENTION

One night, when the Angel Gabriel was in the Sidrah he heard God pronounce the words of consent, and he said to himself: 'A servant of God at this moment invokes the Eternal, but who can he be? I only know that he must be of great merit, that his body of desire is dead and that his spirit is living.' And at once he set off to find this happy mortal. But though he searched the earth and the islands, the mountains and the plains, he could not find him. So he returned to God, and again heard a favourable response to the prayer.

Once more he flew over earth and sea, but at last he had to ask: 'O God, which way will lead me to your servant?' God said: 'Go to the country of Rūm, and in a certain Christian monastery you will find him.' Gabriel flew off to the monastery and there he saw the object of celestial favours bowing before an idol. 'O master of the world,' said Gabriel, 'draw aside the veil from this mystery. How can you answer the prayer of an idol-worshipper in a monastery?' God said: 'His heart is darkened. He is unaware that he has lost his way. Since he strays through ignorance my loving-kindness pardons him and I have opened the way for him to a high estate.' Then the Most High unloosed the man's tongue so that he could pronounce the name of God.

One must not neglect the smallest thing. Renunciation is not bought in a shop; neither can you reach the court of the Most High by paying a small sum.

THE SUFI

As a Sufi was hurrying to Baghdad he heard someone say: 'I have a lot of honey which I would sell very reasonably if there were anyone to buy it.' The Sufi said: 'My good fellow, wouldn't you like to give me a little for nothing?' The man angrily replied: 'Go away. Are you mad as well as greedy? Don't you know that one always gets nothing for nothing?' Then an inner voice said to the Sufi: 'Leave this place and I will give you that which money cannot buy: all good fortune and all that you desire. God's mercy is a burning sun which reaches to the smallest atom. God even rebuked the prophet Moses because of an unbeliever.'

GOD REBUKES MOSES

One day God said to Moses: 'Korah, sobbing, called you seventy times and you did not reply. If he had called me thus, once, I would have wrested his heart from the pit of polytheism and covered his breast with a vestment of faith. O Moses, you have caused him to perish in a hundred agonies, you have cast him into the earth with disgrace. If you had been his creator you would have been less stern with him.'

He who is merciful even to those who are without mercy is highly favoured by compassionate men. If you commit the faults of ordinary sinners you yourself will become one of the wicked.

20

THE QUERY OF THE FOURTH BIRD

Another bird said to the Hoopoe: 'I am effeminate, and can only hop from one branch to another. Sometimes I am wanton and dissolute, at other times I am abstinent. Sometimes my desires drag me to the taverns, sometimes my spirit draws me to prayer. Sometimes, in spite of myself, Satan leads me astray; at other times angels guide me back. Between these two I am in the pit and the prison; what can I do save lament, like Joseph?'

The Hoopoe replied: 'This happens to every man, according to his nature. If we had been guiltless from the beginning God would not have had to send his messengers and prophets. Through obedience you can attain felicity. O you who loll in the sweating room of indolence and yet are full of idle wishes, while you continue to feed the dog of desire your nature is worse than that of an impotent hermaphrodite.'

ANECDOTE OF SHABLI

Shabli once disappeared from Baghdad, no one knew where. At last he was discovered in a house of eunuchs, sitting with humid eye and dry lips among these grotesque creatures. His friends said: 'This is no place for you who are a student of divine mysteries.' He replied: 'These persons, in the way of religion, are neither men nor women. I am as they. I sink in inertia, and my virility is a reproach. If you use praise and blame to make distinctions you are creating idols. When you conceal a hundred idols under your khirka, why appear before men as a Sufi?'

QUARREL OF TWO SUFIS

Two men wearing the khirka of the Sufis were abusing each other before the tribunal. The judge stood them apart and

said: 'It is not becoming for Sufis to dispute among themselves. If you have put on the mantle of resignation why
quarrel? If you are men of violence then throw away your
mantles. But if you are worthy of them be reconciled to each
other. I who am a judge, and not a man of the spiritual way,
am ashamed for the khirka; it would be better to agree to
differ than, while wearing it, to quarrel.'

If you wish to follow the way of love throw your prejudices to the wind and renounce attachment to the things
of the body. Meanwhile, in order not to be a source of evil,
do not give way to resentment and self-love!

THE KING AND THE BEGGAR

Once upon a time in Egypt an unfortunate man fell in love
with the king, who when he heard about it sent for the mis-
guided man and said: 'Since you are in love with me you
must choose one of two things—either have your head cut
off or go into exile.' The man said that he preferred exile,
and almost beside himself, got ready to go. But the king
ordered him to be beheaded. A chamberlain said: 'He is
innocent; why must he die?' 'It is,' said the king, 'because
he is not a true lover and was not whole-hearted. Had he
really desired me, he would rather have lost his head than
leave the object of his love. It would have been all or
nothing. Had he consented to execution, I would have
girded up my loins and become his dervish. He who loves
me, but loves his head better, is no true lover.'

21

EXCUSES OF THE FIFTH BIRD

Another bird said to the Hoopoe: 'I am my own enemy;
there is a thief in me. How can I make this journey hindered
by bodily appetites and a dog of desire which will not
submit? How can I save my soul? The prowling wolf I

know but this dog I do not know, and he is so attractive. I know not where I am with this unfaithful body. Will I ever understand it?'

The Hoopoe replied: 'You yourself are a stray dog, trampled underfoot. This "soul" of yours is one-eyed and squinting; vile, slothful and unfaithful. If a man is drawn to you it is because he is dazzled by the tinsel glitter of your "soul". It is not good for this dog of desire to be pampered and rubbed with oils. As a child, man is weak and heedless; as a youth he is engaged in struggle; and when old age takes possession desire languishes and the body is feeble. Existence being such, how will this dog acquire the ornament of spiritual qualities? From beginning to end we live heedlessly, and obtain nothing. Often a man comes to the end empty, with nothing in him except a desire for the things of exterior life. Thousands perish from grief, but this dog of desire never dies. Listen to the story of a grave-digger who had grown old in his trade. Someone asked him: "Will you answer a question for me since you have spent your whole life digging graves. Tell me if you have ever seen a marvel?" He said: "My dog of desire has seen the dead buried for seventy years, but he himself has not once died, nor for a single moment has he obeyed the laws of God. This is a marvel!"'

AN ANECDOTE OF ABBASAH

One evening, Abbasah said: 'Supposing that the un-believers who fill the earth, and even the loquacious Turkomans, should sincerely accept the Faith—such a thing could be possible. But a hundred and twenty thousand prophets have been sent to the unbelieving soul so that it should accept the Musulmān faith or perish, and they have not yet succeeded. Why so much zeal and so little result?'

We are all under the domination of the Nāfs of this unfaithful disobedient body, which we maintain in ourselves.

Helped as it is from two sides, it were astonishing if this body perished. The Spirit, like a faithful knight, rides on, but always the dog is his companion; he may gallop but the dog follows. The love the heart receives is taken by the body. Yet he who makes himself master of this dog will take in his net the lion of the two worlds.

22

A KING QUESTIONS A DERVISH

A king once saw a man, who, though clad in rags was working in the way of self-perfection. He called him and asked: 'Who is the better off, you or I?' The man said: 'O ignorant one, beat your breast and hold your tongue. Who praises himself does not understand the meaning of words; but this I must say, there can be no doubt that a man such as I is a thousand times better off than a man such as you. With not even the taste of religion, your dog of desire has reduced you to the status of an ass. He is your master and rides you on a bridle pulling your head this way and that. You do all that he commands. You are a non-entity, and fit for nothing, whereas I who know the secrets of the heart have made of this dog, my ass to ride upon. Your dog rules you, but if you will make of it an ass you are then as I, and a hundred times better off than your fellows.'

EXCUSE OF THE SIXTH BIRD

Another bird said to the Hoopoe: 'Whenever I wish to enter the Way the devil rouses my vanity and prevents me from seeking a guide. My heart is troubled, for I have not the strength to resist him. How can I save myself from Iblis and be vivified by the wine of the Spirit?'

The Hoopoe replied: 'So long as the dog of desire runs before you the devil will not leave you, but will use the dog's allurements to mislead you. Then each of your vain desires becomes a demon, and each one yielded to begets a hundred others. This world is a sweating room or prison, the domain of the devil; have no truck with it or with its master.'

COMPLAINT OF A NOVICE ON THE TEMPTATION OF A DEMON

A heedless youth went to one who was fasting to complain of forty temptations of a demon. He said: 'The demon keeps me from the Way, and he has reduced my religion to nothing.' The shaikh said: 'My dear young man, just before you came to me I saw the demon prowling round you. Contrary to what you say he was vexed and was throwing dust on his head because you had ill-treated him and he said to me: "The whole world is my domain but I have no power over him who is the enemy of the world." Tell the demon to pass on, and he will leave you alone.'

THE KHOJA AND THE SUFI

A Sufi heard a Khoja utter this prayer: 'O God have mercy on me and favour my enterprises', and said to him: 'Do not hope for mercy if you have not taken the khirka of a Sufi. You have lifted your face towards heaven and the four golden walls. You are served by ten male and ten female slaves. How shall divine grace come to you in secret? Observe yourself and see if you merit favours. Since you pray for possessions and honours, mercy will hide its face. Turn away from all this, and be free, as are the perfected men.'

23

EXCUSE OF THE SEVENTH BIRD

Another bird said to the Hoopoe: 'I love gold; for me it is like the almond in its shell. If I do not have gold I am bound hand and foot. Love of worldly things and love of gold have filled me with vain desires which blind me to spiritual things.'

The Hoopoe replied: 'O you who are dazzled by exterior forms, in whose heart the value of real things never dawns! You are like a man who can see only in the dark, a nyctalope; you are like an ant, attracted by appearances. Try to understand the sense of things. Without its colour gold would be an ordinary metal; yet you are seduced by colour, like a child. Love of gold is not becoming to a real man; why, they hide it in the vagina of a mule! Does one hide precious things in such a place? If you let no one benefit by your gold you will not profit either. But if you give an obol to some poor wretch, both of you will profit. If you have gold you can benefit many; but if your shoulder is marked, that also is because of gold. For a shop, you must pay rent and sometimes the price is your own soul. You sacrifice everything for your business, even those to whom you are most attached, and in the end you have nothing. We can only hope that fortune will leave a ladder under the gallows. It does not mean that you should make no use at all of the things of the world, but you should spend on all sides that which you possess. Good fortune will come to you only as you give. If you cannot renounce life completely you can at least free yourself from the *love* of riches and honours.'

THE PIR AND HIS COMPANION

A young pupil, unknown to his shaikh (as he thought) had a small hoard of gold pieces. The shaikh said nothing, and one day they set out together on a journey. At length they came to a dark valley at the entrance of which were two roads. The pupil began to be afraid, for gold corrupts its possessor. Trembling, he asked the shaikh, 'Which road ought we to take?' The shaikh replied: 'Get rid of that which makes you afraid, then either road will be good. The

devil fears him who is indifferent to money, and promptly
flees from him. For the sake of a grain of gold you would
split a hair. In the way of religion gold is like a lame donkey;
it has no value, only weight. When wealth comes to a man
unawares it first bewilders him, then governs him. He who
is identified with the love of money and possessions has been
bound hand and foot and thrown into a pit. Avoid this deep
pit if you can, if not, hold your breath, for the air in it is
quite extraordinary.'

GOD REBUKES A DERVISH

A holy man who had found prosperity in God gave himself
up to worship and adoration for forty years. He had fled
from the world, but since God was intimately united to him
he was satisfied. This dervish had enclosed a plot of ground
in the desert; in the middle of it was a tree, and in the tree
a bird had made its nest. The song of the bird was sweet to
hear for in each of its notes were a hundred secrets. The
servant of God was enchanted. But God told a seer about
this state of things in these words: 'Tell this Sufi I am
astonished that after so many years of devotion he has ended
by selling me for a bird. It is true that this bird is admirable,
but its song has caught him in a snare. I have bought him,
and he has sold me.'

24

EXCUSES OF THE EIGHTH BIRD

Another bird said to the Hoopoe: 'My heart is aglow with
pleasure for I live in a charming spot. I have a golden palace,
so beautiful that everyone admires it, and there I exist in a
world of contentment. How can I be expected to give it
up? In this palace I am as a king among birds, why then
should I expose myself to hardships in the valleys of which
you speak? Must I give up both my palace and my royalty?

No reasonable creature would forsake the garden of Irem to undertake so toilsome and difficult a journey!'

The Hoopoe replied: 'O you who are without aspiration and energy! Are you a dog? or do you wish to be an attendant in the hammam? This lower world is only a hot-room and your palace is part of it. Even if your palace is a paradise, nevertheless, death will one day turn it into a prison of suffering. Only if death ceases to exercise his power over creatures would it be expedient for you to remain content in your golden palace.'

A SAGE'S JEST CONCERNING A PALACE

A king built a palace which cost him a hundred thousand dinars. Outside it was adorned with gilded towers and cupolas, and the furniture and carpets made the interior a paradise. When it was finished he invited men from every country to visit him. They came and presented gifts, and he made them all sit down with him. Then he asked them: 'Tell me what you think of my palace. Has anything been forgotten which mars its beauty?' They all protested that never had there been such a palace on earth and never would its like be seen again. All, that is, except one, a Sage, who stood up and said: 'Sire, there is one small crevice which to me seems a blemish. Were it not for this blemish, paradise itself would bring gifts to you from the invisible world.'

'I don't see this blemish,' said the king angrily. 'You are an ignorant person and you only wish to make yourself important.' 'No, proud King,' replied the Sage. 'This chink of which I speak is that through which Azrael, the angel of death, will come. Would to God you could stop it up, for otherwise, what use is your gorgeous palace, your crown and your throne? When death comes they will be as a handful of dust. Nothing lasts, and it is this which spoils the beauty of your dwelling. No art can make stable that which is unstable. Ah, do not put your hopes of happiness upon a palace! Do not let the courser of your pride caracole. If no one dares speak plainly to the king and remind him of his faults, that is a great misfortune.'

THE SPIDER

Have you ever watched the spider and noted how fantastically she spends her time? With speed and foresight she spins her marvellous web, a house which she garnishes for her use. When the fly falls headlong into the web, she rushes up, sucks the little creature's blood and leaves the body to dry for use as food. Then, along comes the householder with a broom, and in an instant web, fly and spider are gone —all three!

The web represents the world; the fly, the subsistence which God has placed there for man. Even if all the world should fall to you, you may lose it in an instant. You are but an infant on the path of understanding; yet you stand trifling outside the curtain. Do not strive after place and position if you have not eaten the brain of an ass. And know, heedless fool, that this world is given over to the bulls. He for whom drums and flags denote high dignity will never become a dervish; these things are but the whistling of the wind, of less value than the smallest coin. Curb the caracoling of the courser of your folly, and do not be deluded by the possession of power. As the panther is flayed, so your life will be snatched away.

Open the eye of true aspiration and discover the spiritual Path; put your feet in the Way of God and seek his celestial court. Once you have glimpsed that you will no longer be attached to the glitter of this world.

THE MISANTHROPIC DERVISH

A man, tired and dispirited, weary with walking in the desert came at last to a place where lived a solitary dervish, and said to him: 'O Dervish, how are things with you?'

The dervish replied: 'Aren't you ashamed to ask such a
question when here I stay in a place so confined and shut
in?' The man said: 'That isn't true. How can you be shut in,
living in this vast desert?' The dervish added: 'If the world
were not so small, you never would have lighted on me!'

25

EXCUSE OF THE NINTH BIRD

Another bird said to the Hoopoe: 'O most eminent bird, I
am the slave of a charming being who has taken possession
of me and deprived me of my reason. The image of her dear
face is a thief of the great Path; she has put fire to the harvest
of my life, and when I am absent from her I have not a
moment's peace. Since my heart is on fire with passion I do
not see how I can set out on this journey. I should have to
cross the valleys and go through a hundred trials. Can I be
expected to forsake this beauty to travel through scorching
heat and bitter cold? I am too weak to go without her; and
I am but the dust on her road. Such is my state. What can
I do?'

The Hoopoe replied: 'You are attached to visible things,
and are head and foot in the suffering which follows from
this. Sensual love is a game. Love which is inspired by
passing beauty is itself fleeting. You are always comparing
a body of blood and moods to the beauty of the moon.
What is uglier than a body composed of flesh and bones?
True beauty is hidden. Seek it then, in the invisible world.
If the veil which hides the mysteries from our eyes should
fall, nothing would be left in the world. All visible forms
would be reduced to nothing.'

AN ANECDOTE OF SHABLI

A man came to Shabli one day, weeping. The Sufi asked him
why he wept. 'O Shaikh,' he said, 'I had a friend whose

beauty made my soul as verdant as branches in spring. Yesterday, he died, and I too shall die of sorrow.' Shabli said: 'Why do you grieve? For a long time you have had his friendship. Go now and choose another friend, one who will not die, then you will not lay up for yourself a cause for grief. Attachment to a mortal can only bring sorrow.'

THE RICH MERCHANT

A merchant rich in goods and money had a slave who was sweet as sugar. Nevertheless, he decided one day to sell her. But it was not long before he began to miss her. In his longing he went to the new master and begged him to let her go, and offered a thousand pieces of gold to buy her back. But he refused to part with her. So the merchant went out, and throwing dust on his head said: 'It is my own fault, for having sewn up my lips and my eye; in my greed I have sold my mistress for a piece of gold. It was a bad day for me when I dressed her up in her best attire and took her to the bazaar to sell for a good profit.'

Each of your breaths, which measure your existence, is a pearl, and each of your atoms is a guide to God. The benefits of this friend cover you from head to foot. If you were truly aware of him how could you support the separation?

ANECDOTE OF HALLĀJ

When they were about to impale Hallāj, he only uttered these words: 'I am God.' They cut off his hands and feet so that he became pale from loss of blood. Then he drew the stumps of his wrists across his face saying: 'It will not do for me to look pale today or they will think I am afraid. I will redden my face so that when the bloody man who has carried out the sentence turns towards the gibbet, he will see that I am a brave man.'

He who eats and sleeps in the month of July with the dragon of seven heads will fare very badly in such a game, but the gibbet will be a very small thing for him.

26

EXCUSE OF THE TENTH BIRD

This bird said to the Hoopoe: 'I am afraid of death. Now this valley is wide, and I have nothing at all for the journey. I am so filled with the fear of death that my life will leave me at the first stopping place. Even were I a powerful emir, in the hour of death I should fear no less. He who with a sword would try to ward off death, shall have it broken like a Kalam; for alas, faith in the strength of the hand and of the sword brings only disappointment and sorrow.'

The Hoopoe replied: 'O you who are fickle and weak-willed, do you wish to remain a mere frame of bone and marrow? Don't you know that life, be it long or short, is composed of a few breaths? Don't you understand that whoever is born must also die? That he goes into the earth and that the wind disperses the elements of which his body was made?

'You were nourished for death; and you were brought into the world in order to be taken away from it! The sky is like a dish upside down, which every evening is immersed in the blood of sunset. One could say that the sun, armed with a scimitar, is cutting off heads on this dish. Whether you be good or bad you are only a drop of water kneaded with earth. Though all your life you may have been in a position of authority, you will, in the end, give up the ghost in affliction.'

THE PHOENIX

The Phoenix is an admirable and lovely bird which lives in Hindustan. It has no mate and lives alone. Its beak, which is very long and hard, is pierced like a flute with nearly a hundred holes. Each of these holes gives out a sound and in each sound is a particular secret. Sometimes he makes music through the holes, and when the birds and the fishes hear his sweet plaintive notes they are agitated, and the most ferocious beasts are in rapture; then they all become silent. A philosopher once visited this bird and learnt from him the science of music. The Phoenix lives about a thousand years and he knows exactly the day of his death. When his time comes he gathers round him a quantity of palm leaves and, distraught among the leaves, utters plaintive cries. From the openings in his beak he sends forth varied notes, and this music is drawn from the depths of his heart. His lamentations express the sorrow of death, and he trembles like a leaf. At the sound of his trumpet the birds and the beasts draw near to assist at the spectacle. Now they fall into bewilderment, and many die because their strength fails them. While the Phoenix still has breath, he beats his wings and ruffles his feathers, and by this produces fire. The fire spreads to the palm fronds, and soon both the fronds and the bird are reduced to living coals and then to ashes. But when the last spark has flickered out a new small Phoenix arises from the ashes.

Has it ever happened to anyone to be re-born after death? Even if you lived as long as the Phoenix, nevertheless you would die when the measure of your life was taken. His thousand years of life are filled with lamentations and he remains alone without companions or children, and has contact with no one. When the end comes he throws his ashes to the wind so that you may know that none can escape death whatever trick he may use. Learn then from the miracle of the Phoenix. Death is a tyrant, but we must always keep death in mind. And, although we have much to endure, it is nothing compared with dying.

COUNSEL OF TAI WHEN DYING

When Tai lay dying someone asked him: 'O Tai, you have seen the essence of things, how is it with you now?' He said: 'I can say nothing about my state. I have measured the wind all the days of my life, and now the end is come I shall be buried, and so, good night.'

There is no other remedy for death than to look death constantly in the face. We all are born to die; life will not stay with us; we must submit. Even he who held the world under the seal of his ring is now only a mineral in the earth.

JESUS AND THE PITCHER OF WATER

Jesus drank of the water of a limpid rill whose taste was more agreeable than the dew of the rose. One of his companions filled a pitcher from this rill, and they went on their way. Jesus, being thirsty, took a sip of water from the pitcher, but the water was bitter, and he stopped in astonishment and prayed: 'O God, the water of the rill and the water in the pitcher are the same. Tell me why the one is sweeter than honey and the other so bitter?' The pitcher then spoke, and said to Jesus: 'I am very old, and I have been fashioned over a thousand times under the firmament of the nine cupolas—sometimes as a vase, sometimes as a pitcher, sometimes as a ewer. Whatever form I took I have always had in me the bitterness of death. I am so made that the water I hold will always partake of that bitterness.'

O heedless man! Try to understand the meaning of the pitcher. Strive to discover the mystery before life is taken from you. If while living you fail to find yourself, to know yourself, how will you be able to understand the secret of your existence when you die? You participate in the life of man yet you are only a psuedo man.

SOCRATES TO HIS DISCIPLES

When Socrates was about to die, one of his pupils said to him: 'My master, when we have washed you and put on your shroud where do you want us to bury you?' Socrates said: 'If you find me, dear pupil, bury me where you will, and good night! Seeing that in my long life I have not found myself, how will you find me when I am dead? I have lived in such a manner that at this moment I only know that the least hair of knowledge of myself is not evident.'

27

EXCUSE OF THE ELEVENTH BIRD

Another bird said to the Hoopoe: 'O you whose faith is sincere, I have not a breath of good will. I have spent my life in vexation, desiring the ball of the world. There is such a sadness in my heart that I never cease to mourn. I am always in a state of bewilderment and impotence; and when for a moment I have been content, then am I unbelieving. In consequence, I have become a dervish. But now I hesitate to start out on the road of spiritual knowledge. If my heart were not so full of sorrow I would be charmed with this journey. As it is I am in a state of perplexity. Now that I have put my case before you tell me what I ought to do.'

The Hoopoe said: 'You, who are given over to pride, who are swallowed up in self-pity, you do well to be disturbed. Seeing that the world passes, you yourself should pass it by. Abandon it, for whoever becomes identified with transient things can have no part in the things that are lasting. The sufferings you endure can be made glorious and not humiliating. That which in outward appearance is suffering can be a treasure for the seer. A hundred blessings will come to you if you make effort on the Path. But as you are, you are only a skin covering a dull brain.'

THE GRATEFUL SLAVE

One day a good-natured king gave a rare and beautiful fruit to a slave, who tasted it and thereupon said that never in his life had he eaten anything so delicious. This made the king wish to try it himself, and he asked the slave for a piece. But when he put it into his mouth he found it very bitter and he raised his eyebrows in astonishment. The slave said: 'Sire, since I have received so many gifts at your hand how can I complain of one bitter fruit? Seeing that you shower benefits on me why should one bitterness estrange me from you?'

So, servant of God, if you experience suffering in your striving, be persuaded that it can be a treasure for you. The thing seems topsy-turvy but, remember the slave.

THE SHAIKH AND THE OLD WOMAN

An old woman said to Shaikh Mahmāh: 'Teach me a prayer so that I may find contentment. So far I have always been a prey to discontent, but I now wish to be free.'

The shaikh replied: 'A long time ago I withdrew into a sort of fortress behind my knee to seek ardently that which you desire; but I have neither felt it nor seen it. So long as we do not accept everything in the way of love, how can we be content?'

A QUESTION TO JUNAID

Someone asked Junaid: 'Slave of God who yet are free, tell me how to reach a state of contentment?' Junaid replied: 'When one has learned, through love, to accept.'

The atom has only an apparent brilliance. By nature it is only an atom, but if it loses itself in the sun, it will thereby share his quality for ever.

THE BAT IN SEARCH OF THE SUN

One night a bat was heard to say: 'How is it that I am unable even for a moment to see the sun? All my life I have been in despair because not for an instant can I be lost in him. For months and years I have flown hither and thither with my eyes shut, and here I am!' A contemplative said: 'You are beset with pride, and you still have thousands of years to travel. How can such a being as you discover the sun? Can an ant reach the moon?' 'Nevertheless,' said the bat, 'I shall still go on trying.' And so for some years it continued to search until it had neither strength nor wings. As it still had not discovered the sun it said: 'Perhaps I have flown beyond it.' A wise bird hearing this, said: 'You live in a dream; you have been going round in circles, and haven't advanced a single step; and in your pride you say you have gone beyond the sun!' This so shocked the bat that realizing her helplessness she humbled herself completely, saying: 'You have found a bird with inner sight, go no further.'

28

QUESTION OF THE TWELFTH BIRD

Another bird said to the Hoopoe: 'O you, who are our guide, what will be the result if I surrender my will to you? I cannot of my own will accept the toil and suffering that I know I shall have to undergo, but I can agree to obey your commands; and if I should chance to turn my head away I will make amends.'

The Hoopoe replied: 'You have spoken well, one cannot expect better than this. For how can you remain master of yourself if you follow your likes and dislikes? But if you obey voluntarily you may become your own master. He who submits to obedience on this path is delivered from deception and escapes many difficulties. One hour of serving God in accordance with the true law is worth a lifetime of serving the world. He who accepts passive suffering is like

a stray dog which has to obey the whim of every passer-by.
But he who endures even a moment of active suffering on
this path is fully recompensed.'

BĀYĀZID AND TARMĀZĪ

A learned doctor, a pivot of the world and blessed with
excellent qualities, recounted the following: 'One night,' he
said, 'I saw in a dream Bāyāzid and Tarmāzī, who begged
me to be their leader. I wondered very much why these two
eminent shaikhs treated me with such deference. Then I
remembered that one morning I had heaved a sigh from the
depths of my heart, and as the sigh went up it swung the
hammer of the gate of the sanctuary, so that it was opened
for me. I went in, and all the spiritual masters and their
disciples, speaking without words, asked something of me—
all except Bāyāzid Bistāmī who wished to meet me but not
to ask anything. He said: "When I heard the summons of
your heart I realized that all I need is to obey your orders, to
be guided by your will. Since I am nothing, who am I to say
what I wish? It is enough for the servant to comply with the
wishes of his master."

'This is why the shaikhs have treated me with respect, and
given me precedence. When a man walks in obedience he
acts conformably with the word of God. He is no servant
of God who boasts of being one. The true servant shows
his quality in the time of ordeal. Submit then, to trials, so
that you may know yourself.'

THE SLAVE AND THE ROBE OF HONOUR

A king gave a robe of honour to a slave, who went away
very pleased with himself. As he walked along, the dust of
the street settled on him, and he thoughtlessly wiped his
face with the sleeve of the robe. One who was jealous of him

lost no time in informing the king, who, indignant at this breach of good manners, had him impaled.

He who dishonours himself by unseemly conduct is not worthy to wait on the carpet of a king.

29

REQUEST OF THE THIRTEENTH BIRD

Another bird asked the Hoopoe: 'O you whose motives are without guile, tell me how I can be sincere on this path to God. Since I cannot give up the longing of my heart I spend all that I have to achieve my aim. What I had I lost; what I kept has turned to scorpions in my hands. I am bound by no ties and have cast off all shackles and impediments. I wish to be sincere in the spiritual Way in the hope of one day seeing the object of my worship face to face.'

The Hoopoe replied: 'The Way is not open to everyone; only the upright may tread it. He who strives in this Way must do so tranquilly and with a whole heart. When you have burnt all that you possess gather the ashes together and seat yourself upon them. Until you die to all the things of this world, one by one, you will not be free. And seeing that you will not be long in the prison of the world detach yourself from everything. When death comes, can the things that now enslave you turn him aside? To travel this road, self-sincerity is necessary—and to be sincere with oneself is more difficult than you think.'

ALLEGORICAL SAYING OF TARMĀZĪ

The saint of Turkestan said one day to himself: 'I love two things, my son and my piebald horse. If I should hear that my son had died I would surrender my horse as a thanksgiving, for these two things are as idols to my soul.'

Set light to your faults, your resentments, and your
vanities. Burn them and do not flatter yourself that you are
more sincere than others. He who prides himself on his
sincerity should strive to see himself as he is.

THE SHAIKH KHIRCĀNI AND THE AUBERGINE

One day Shaikh Khircāni, who rested upon the very throne
of God, had an intense longing for an aubergine. He called
for it with horn and voice, so his mother went out and got
one. No sooner had he eaten it than it happened that they
cut off the head of his child, and at night a wicked man
placed it on his doorstep. The shaikh then said: 'A hundred
times I had a foreboding that if I ate so much as a small piece
of aubergine something disastrous would happen. But the
desire for it was so strong that I could not overcome it.'

He who allows his desires to master him stifles his own
soul. The learned know nothing; there is no surety in their
learning; and many sorts of knowledge are required. At any
moment a new caravan may arrive and a new test.

I know of no one so fortunate as Pharaoh's magicians,
who, with the faith of men today, separated their souls from
themselves; and, grounded in religion, relinquished all love
for things of the world.

30

THE FOURTEENTH BIRD SPEAKS

Another bird said to the Hoopoe: 'O you who are clear-
seeing! This that you propose is a worthy aspiration. Though
I appear to be weak, in reality I have a noble ardour; though
I have little strength, I have a lofty ambition.'

The Hoopoe replied: 'If you have but a little of this noble
ambition, it will triumph even over the sun. Aspiration is
the wings and feathers of the bird of the soul.'

THE OLD WOMAN WHO WISHED TO BUY JOSEPH

It is said that when they sold Joseph to the Egyptians the latter treated him kindly. There were many buyers so the merchants priced him at from five to ten times his weight in musk. Meanwhile, in a state of agitation, an old woman ran up, and going among the buyers said to an Egyptian: 'Let me buy the Canaanite, for I long to possess that young man. I have spun ten spools of thread to pay for him so take them and give me Joseph and say no more about it.'

The merchants smiled and said: 'Your simplicity has misled you. This unique pearl is not for you; they have already offered a hundred treasures for him. How can you bid against them with your spools of thread?' The old woman, looking into their faces, said: 'I know very well that you will not sell him for so little, but it is enough for me that my friends and enemies will say, "this old woman has been among those who wished to buy Joseph".'

He who is without aspiration will never reach the boundless kingdom. Possessed of this lofty ambition a great prince regarded his worldly kingdom as ashes. When he realized the emptiness of temporal royalty, he decided that spiritual royalty was worth a thousand kingdoms of the world.

IBRĀHĪM ADHAM

A man was always complaining of the bitterness of poverty, so Ibrāhīm Adham said to him: 'My son, perhaps you have not paid for your poverty?' The man replied: 'What you say is nonsense, how can one buy poverty?' 'I at least,' said Adham, 'have chosen it voluntarily and I have bought it at the price of the kingdom of the world. And I would still buy a moment of this poverty for a hundred of those worlds.'

Men who have a thirst for self-perfection stake both soul and body on the issue. The bird of aspiration soars to God, lifted on the wings of faith above things temporal and spiritual. If you have not this aspiration it is better to withdraw.

THE WORLD ACCORDING TO A SUFI

A Sufi woke one night and said to himself: 'It seems to me that the world is like a chest in which we are put and the lid shut down, and we give ourselves up to foolishness. When death lifts the lid, he who has acquired wings, soars away to eternity, but he who has not, stays in the chest a prey to a thousand tribulations. Make sure then that the bird of ambition acquires wings of aspiration, and give to your heart and reason the ecstasy of the soul. Before the lid of the chest is opened become a bird of the Spirit, ready to spread your wings.'

31

THE QUERY OF THE FIFTEENTH BIRD

Another bird said to the Hoopoe: 'If the King of whom we speak is just and faithful, God has given us, also, uprightness and integrity; and I have never been lacking in justice towards anyone. When these qualities are found in a man how will he rank in the knowledge of spiritual things?'

The Hoopoe replied: 'Justice is the king of salvation. He who is just is saved from all kinds of errors and futilities. It is better to be just than to pass your whole life in the genuflexions and prostrations of exterior worship. Even liberality is not equal in the two worlds to justice exercised in secret; but he who professes justice openly will find it difficult not to become a hypocrite. As for men of the spiritual Way they ask justice of no one but they receive it generously from God.'

ANECDOTE OF THE IMĀM HAMBAL

Ahmad Hambal was the Imām of his time, and his merit beyond praise. Once when he wished to rest from his studies

and his position he went out to talk with a man who was
very poor. Someone who saw him blamed him saying:
'There is no one more learned than you, and you have no
need of another man's opinions, yet you spend your time
with a poor wretch who goes barefoot and bareheaded.' 'It
is true,' said the Imām, 'that I have carried off the polo ball
in the hadis and the sunna, and that I have more knowledge
than this man; but in regard to understanding he is nearer
to God than I am.'

You who are unjust through ignorance, reflect, at least
for a moment, on the integrity of those who are on the path
of the spirit.

THE INDIAN RAJAH

Sultan Mahmūd once took prisoner an old rajah, who,
experiencing the love of God, became a Musulmān and
renounced the two worlds. Sitting alone in his tent he
became quite absorbed by this, weeping bitter tears and
heaving sighs of longing—in the day more than in the
night, and in the night more than in the day. At last Mahmūd
heard of this and summoned him: 'Do not weep and lament,'
he said, 'you are a Rajah and I will give you a hundred
kingdoms for the one you have lost.' 'O Padishah,' replied
the Hindu, 'I do not weep for my lost kingdom or my
dignity. I weep, because on the day of resurrection, God,
the possessor of glory, will say to me: "O disloyal man, you
have sown against me the grain of insult. Before Mahmūd
attacked you, you never thought of me. Only when you had
to bring your army against him and lost everything did you
remember me. Do you think this is just?" O, young king,
it is because I am ashamed that I weep in my old age.'

Listen to the words of justice and faith; listen to the
teaching in the Diwan of the Sacred Books. If you have
faith, then undertake the journey to which I invite you.

But shall he who is not in the index of fidelity be found in
the chapter of generosity!

THE MUSLIM WARRIOR
AND
THE CHRISTIAN CRUSADER

A Muslim and a Christian were fighting, and the moment
arrived for the Muslim to say his appointed prayers, so he
proudly demanded a respite from the Christian. The
crusader agreed, so the Muslim went aside and said his
prayers. When he returned they resumed the combat with
renewed vigour. A little later the crusader in his turn asked
for a truce to say his prayers. This being granted he withdrew himself, and choosing a suitable spot, bowed in the
dust before his idol. When the Musulmān saw his adversary
with his head bowed he said to himself: 'Now is my chance
to gain the victory,' thinking to strike him down by
treachery. But an inner voice said: 'O faithless man to betray
your pledge, is this how you keep your word? The unbeliever did not draw his sword against you when you
asked for a truce. Do you not remember the words of the
Koran: "Keep your promises faithfully." Since an unbeliever has been generous to you, be not wanting in regard
to him. He has done well, you wish to do ill. Do to him
as he has done to you. Are you, a Musulmān, not to be
worthy of trust?' At this, the Musulmān halted. Remorse
overcame him and he was bathed in tears from head to foot.
When the crusader noticed this he asked the reason. 'A
heavenly voice,' said the Musulmān, 'reproached me for not
keeping faith with you. You see me in this state because I
have been vanquished by your generosity.' At this the
Christian gave a great cry, and said: 'Since God can show
favour to me, his guilty enemy, and rebuke his friend for
being faithless, how can I abide in infidelity? Expound to

me the principles of Islam so that I may accept the true faith
and casting polytheism behind me adopt the rites of the law.
Oh, how I regret the blindness that has hindered me until
now from acknowledging such a Master.'

O you who have neglected to seek the true object of your
desires, and are grossly lacking in the faith which is his due!
I think the time will come when in your presence heaven
will recall all your acts one by one.

JOSEPH AND HIS BRETHREN

In the time of the famine, the ten brothers of Joseph made
the long journey to Egypt. Joseph received them, his face
covered with a veil, and they recounted their hardships and
asked for help against the terrors of famine.

In front of Joseph was a cup, which he struck with his
hand, and it gave out a mournful sound. The brothers were
in a state of consternation: they loosened their tongues and
said to him: 'O Aziz! Do you, or does anyone, know what
this sound signifies?' 'I know very well,' said Joseph, 'but
you will not be able to bear the telling of it; for the cup says
that you had a brother, who was remarkable for his beauty,
and whose name was Joseph.'

Then Joseph struck the cup a second time and said: 'The
cup tells me that you threw him into a well and that you
killed an innocent wolf and stained Joseph's coat with the
blood.'

Joseph struck the cup a third time, and again it gave out
a mournful sound. He added: 'The cup says that Joseph's
brothers plunged their father into the depths of grief and
that they have sold Joseph.

'Now what have these unbelievers done with their
brother? Fear God, at least, you who stand before me.'

This put them into such a state that they sweated with
fear, they, who had come to ask for bread. In selling Joseph

they had sold themselves; when they put him in the well they themselves were cast into a pit of affliction.

He who reads this story without profit is blind. Do not listen with indifference, for this is none other than your own story. You continue to commit sins and faults because you have not been lighted with the light of understanding. If someone strikes the cup of your life, then unveil to yourself your guilty deeds. When the cup of your life is struck and you wake from sleep; when your injustices and sins are exposed one by one, I doubt if you will keep your peace or your reason. You are like a lame ant in a bowl. How often have you turned your head from the cup of heaven? Spread your wings and fly upward, you, who have a knowledge of the truth. If not, you will always be ashamed when you hear the sound of the cup.

32

QUESTION OF THE SIXTEENTH BIRD

Another bird asked the Hoopoe: 'O you who are our leader, is boldness permitted in approaching the Majesty of the Simurgh? It seems to me that he who has courage is freed from many fears. Since you are such, scatter pearls of wisdom and tell us the secret.'

'Everyone who is worthy,' replied the Hoopoe, 'is the Mahrām of the secret of divinity, and it is good to be bold if one has intelligence of the secrets of God. But how can one who possesses the secrets impart them to another? Can a camel-driver of the desert be the confidant of a king? Still, if one is actuated by pure love a little boldness is permitted. He who is on the path of self-knowledge should know when to be bold, and not let himself die from lack of effort.

'A true dervish will be bold and confident from the true hope he experiences. He who is fearless from love sees the

Lord in all. His boldness then is good and laudable, because he is an idiot of love, on fire.'

AN IDIOT OF GOD AND THE SLAVES OF AMĪD

Khorassan was in a state of prosperity because of the wise rule of Prince Amīd. He was attended by a hundred Turkish slaves whose countenances shone like the full moon, their bodies were slender cypresses, their legs as silver, and their breath was musk. They wore ear-rings of pearl whose reflection lighted up the night and made it seem as day; their turbans were of the finest brocade, and round their necks were collars of gold; their breasts were covered with silver cloth, and their belts enriched with precious stones. All were mounted on white horses. Whoever looked at one of them lost his heart at once. By chance, a Sufi, clothed in rags and barefoot, saw this body of young men in the distance, and asked: 'What is this cavalcade of houris?' He was told, 'These young men are the pages of Amīd, the prince of this city.' When the idiot of God heard this, the vapour of folly went to his head and he cried: 'O God, the possessor of the glorious canopy, teach Amīd to take care of his servants.'

If you are like this idiot, have also his boldness; lift yourself up like a slender tree; but if you have no leaves do not be daring and do not jest. The daring of the fools of God is a good thing. They cannot tell if the way is good or bad, they only know how to act.

A HOLY FOOL

The Hoopoe continued: 'An idiot of God went naked and starving along the road in winter. With neither house nor shelter he was soaked with rain and sleet. At last he came to a ruined palace and decided to take refuge there, but as he went in at the doorway a tile fell on his head and cracked his skull, so that the blood flowed. He turned his face to heaven and said: "Wouldn't it be better to beat the royal drum than to drop a tile on my head?"'

PRAYER OF A MADMAN

There was a famine in Egypt, so dreadful that everywhere people were dying as they begged for bread. By chance a madman passed along and seeing how many were perishing of starvation he said to God: 'O you who possess the good things of the world and of religion, since you cannot feed all men, create fewer.'

If one who would be bold in the court should say something unbecoming, he must humbly ask for forgiveness.

ANOTHER FOOL

A Sufi, an idiot of God, was tormented by children who threw stones at him. At last he took refuge in a corner of a building. But at that moment it began to hail and the hailstones came through an open skylight and fell on his head. The man took the hail for pebbles and began to stretch out his tongue and insult the children, whom he imagined were throwing them, for the house was dark. At length he discovered that the pebbles were only hailstones, and he was sorry and prayed: 'O God, it was because the house was dark that I have sinned with my tongue.'

If you understand the motives of those who are in darkness, you will, no doubt, forgive them.

33

THE SEVENTEENTH BIRD QUESTIONS THE HOOPOE

Another bird said to the Hoopoe: 'As long as I live the love of the Eternal Being will be dear and agreeable to me, and I shall never cease to think of him. I have been about with all living creatures and far from being attached to them I am identified with none. The folly of love occupies all my thoughts, so for me, love is enough. But such love is not expedient for everyone, and now the time has come when I must draw a line on my life so that I shall be able to take a cup of wine from my beloved; then the eye of my heart will be rendered luminous by his beauty, and my hand will touch his neck as a pledge of the union.'

The Hoopoe replied: 'It is not by these pretentious boastings that one can become an honoured guest of the Simurgh of the Caucasus. Do not extol so much the love that you believe you feel for him, for it is not given to everyone to possess it. It is necessary that the wind of good fortune should lift the veil of the mystery, then the Simurgh will draw you to him and you shall sit with him in his harem. If you wish to come to the sacred place you must first of all strive to have a knowledge of spiritual things, otherwise your love for the Simurgh will be turned to torment. For your true felicity it is necessary that the Simurgh shall also love you.'

DREAM OF A DISCIPLE OF BĀYĀZID

When Bāyāzid departed from the palace of this world a disciple saw him the same night in a dream and asked this excellent pīr how he had escaped Munkir and Nakir. The Sufi said to him: 'When these two angels questioned me about the Creator, I said to them, "The question cannot be answered precisely, for if I say 'he is my God, and that is all', this will only express a desire on my part; it will be better if you return to God and ask him what he thinks of *me*. If he calls me his servant, you will know that it is so. If not, then he abandons me to the bonds which hold me. Since it is not easy to obtain union with God, what will it serve me to call him My Lord? If he does not agree to my

service how can I claim him for my master? It is true that
I have bowed my head, but it is also necessary that he calls
me his slave."'

MAHMŪD IN THE HOT-ROOM OF THE HAMMAM

One night, Mahmūd, being in a state of dejection, went in
disguise to the hammam. A young attendant welcomed him
and made the necessary arrangements for him to sweat
comfortably over the hot coals. Afterwards he gave the
Sultan some dry bread, which he ate. Then the Sultan said
to himself: 'If this attendant had excused himself from
receiving me I would have had his head cut off.' At last the
Sultan told the young man that he wished to return to his
palace. The young man said: 'You have eaten my food,
you have known my bed, and you have been my guest. I
shall always be glad to receive you. Though in reality we
are made of the same substance, how, in regard to outer
things, can you be compared to one in my lowly position?'
The Sultan was so pleased with this answer that he went
seven times more as the guest of the attendant. On the last
occasion he told him to make a request. 'If I, a beggar,
should make a request,' the attendant said, 'the Sultan will
not grant it.' 'Ask what you will,' said the Sultan, 'even if it
be to leave the hammam and become a king.' 'My only
request,' said he, 'is that the Sultan shall continue to be my
guest. To be a bath attendant sitting near you in a hot room
is better than to be a king in a garden without you. Since
good fortune has come to me because of the hot-room, it
would be ungrateful of me to leave it. Your presence has
lighted up this place; what can I ask for better than yourself?'

If you love God seek also to be loved by him. But while
one man seeks this love, ever old and ever new, another
desires two obols of silver from the treasure of the world;
he seeks a drop of water when he might have the ocean.

THE TWO WATER-CARRIERS

A water-carrier, meeting another, asked him for some of his water. The latter said: 'O you who are ignorant of spiritual things, why don't you drink your own?' The first said: 'Give me some of your water, you who have spiritual knowledge, for I am sick of my own.'

Adam was satiated with familiar things, and that is why he brought himself to take the wheat, a new thing for him. He sold the old things for a little wheat. He became one-eyed. Love came and knocked at the door for him. When he was completely destroyed in the lightning of love, both old and new things disappeared and nothing was left! But it is not given to everyone to be disgusted with himself and to die completely to his old life.

34

SPEECH OF THE EIGHTEENTH BIRD

Another bird said to the Hoopoe: 'I believe that I have acquired for myself all the perfection that is possible, and I have acquired it by painful austerities. Since I have obtained here the result that I wish, it is difficult for me to set out for this place you speak of. Have you ever known anyone leave a treasure to go painfully wandering over the mountains, in the wilderness, and across the plains?'

The Hoopoe replied: 'O diabolical creature, full of conceit and self-pride! You who are sunk in egoism! You who have such an aversion to doing! You have been seduced by your imagination and you are now far from divine things. The body of desire has the upper hand of your spirit; the devil has stolen your brain. Pride has taken possession of you. The light you think you have in the Spiritual Way is only a flickering flame. Your taste for heavenly things is imaginary. Do not let yourself be seduced by the glimmer which you see. So long as your body of desire confronts you, be aware of yourself. You must fight this enemy, sword in hand. When a false light shows itself from your body of desire you must look on it as the sting of a scorpion, for which you must use parsley. Do not despair because of the obscurity of the way which I shall show you, and because the light that you will see there will give you no pretension to be a companion of the sun. So long as you continue to live, O my dear, in the pride of life, your readings of books and your puny efforts are not worth an obol. Only when you give up this pride and vanity will you be able to leave this exterior life without regret. So long as you hold on to conceit and self-pride and the things of outer life, a hundred arrows of vexation will pierce you from every side.'

SHAIKH ABŪ BEKR OF NISHAPŪR

The shaikh went out one day from his monastery in the company of his disciples, riding on his donkey while his companions followed walking. All at once the donkey broke wind with a loud noise, whereupon the shaikh gave a cry and tore his khirka. His disciples looked at him in surprise, and one of them asked him why he acted like this. He said: 'When I looked round and saw the number of my followers I thought to myself, "Now am I really equal to Bāyāzid. Today, I am accompanied by many earnest disciples; so, tomorrow, I shall without doubt ride with glory and honour over the plain of the resurrection."' He added, 'It was then, when I presumed this to be my destiny, that my donkey made that seemingly incongruous noise you heard. By this he wished to say, "Here is the reply that an ass makes to him who has such pretensions, and thoughts so vain!" That is why the fire of repentance fell so suddenly on my soul,

and why my attitude has changed, and my imaginary position has fallen to pieces.'

O you who change with every moment, you are as
Pharaoh to the roots of your hair. But if you destroy in
yourself the ego for a single day, your darkness will be
lighted up. Never say the word 'I'. You, because of your
'I's', are fallen into a hundred evils, and you will always be
tempted of the devil.

GOD SPEAKS TO MOSES

God one day said to Moses in secret: 'Go and get a word of
advice from Satan.' So Moses went to visit Iblis and when
he came to him asked him for a word of advice. 'Always
remember,' said Iblis, 'this simple axiom: never say "I", so
that you never may become like me.'

So long as there remains in you a little of self-love you
will partake of infidelity. Indolence is a barrier to the
spiritual way; but if you succeed in crossing this barrier a
hundred 'I's' will break their heads in a moment.

Everyone sees your vanity and self-pride, your resentment,
envy, and anger, but you yourself do not see them. There is
a corner of your being full of dragons, and by negligence
you are delivered up to them; and you pet them and cherish
them night and day. So, if you are aware of your inner state,
why do you remain so listless!

THE DERVISH WHO POSSESSED A BEAUTIFUL
BEARD

In the time of Moses there was a dervish who spent days
and nights in a state of adoration, yet experienced no feeling
for spiritual things. He had a beautiful long beard, and
often while praying would stop to comb it. One day, seeing
Moses, he went to him and said: 'O Pasha of Mount Sinai,

ask God, I pray you, to tell me why I experience neither spiritual satisfaction nor ecstasy.'

The next time Moses went up on Sinai he spoke to God about the dervish, and God said, in a tone of displeasure: 'Although this dervish has sought union with me, nevertheless he is constantly thinking about his long beard.' When Moses came down he told the Sufi what God had said. The Sufi thereupon began tearing out his beard, weeping bitterly. Gabriel then came along to Moses and said: 'Even now your Sufi is thinking about his beard. He thought of nothing else while praying, and is even more attached to it while he is tearing it out!'

O you who think you have ceased to be pre-occupied with your beard, you are plunged in an ocean of affliction. When you can regard it with detachment you will have a right to sail across this ocean. But if you plunge in with your beard you will have difficulty in getting out.

ANOTHER ANECDOTE OF A MAN WITH A LONG BEARD

A sot, who had a fine long beard, accidentally fell into deep water. A passer-by seeing this, called out: 'Throw away the wallet from your head.' The drowning man replied, 'This is not a wallet, it is my beard, and it is not this which cramps me.' The passer-by said, 'Anyway, let go of it, or you will drown.'

O you who are like goats, and have no shame of your beards, so long as you have a body of desire and a demon to truss you up, the pride of Pharaoh and Haman will be your portion. Turn your back on the world as Moses did and then you will be able to seize this Pharaoh by the beard and hold him firm. He who travels on the path of self-striving must regard his heart only as shish kabab. The man with the watering-pot does not wait for the rain to fall.

35

THE QUERY OF THE NINETEENTH BIRD

Another bird said to the Hoopoe: 'Tell me, you who are celebrated throughout the world, what must I do to be contented on this journey? If you tell me, my mind will be easier, and I shall be willing to be led in this enterprise. In fact, direction is necessary, so that one does not become apprehensive. Since I only wish to accept the direction of the invisible world I repel, with good reason, the false direction of earthly creatures.'

'As long as you live,' replied the Hoopoe, 'be content to remember God, and be on the watch against indiscreet talk. If you can do this the cares and sorrows of your soul will vanish. Live in God in contentment; turn like the dome of heaven for love of him. If you know of anything better, tell it, O poor bird, so that you may be happy for at least a moment.'

ANECDOTE OF A FRIEND OF GOD

A friend of God who was dying began to weep and those with him asked why. 'I weep as the spring clouds,' he said, 'because the time has come when I should die and I am disturbed. Seeing that my heart is already with God how can I die?' One of those present said: 'Since your heart is with God you will die a good death.' The Sufi replied, 'How can death come to him who is united to God! As I am already with him, my death appears to be impossible.'

He who is content to exist as a particle of the great whole loses his egoism and becomes free. Be in contentment with your friend, like the rose in the calyx.

ALLEGORICAL ANECDOTE

A perfected man said: 'For seventy years I have worked on myself and I am now in ecstasy, contentment, and felicity, and in this state I participate in the Sovereign Majesty and am united with Divinity itself. As for you, while you are occupied with looking for the faults of others, how will you be able to taste the joy of the unseen world? If you look for faults with a searching eye, how will you be able to see the things of the inner world? You would split a hair for the faults of others, but to your own faults you turn a blind eye. Acknowledge your own faults, then, guilty though you be, God will have mercy on you.'

THE TWO DRUNKEN MEN

A man who drank too much of that which is limpid, often came to the point when he lost both his senses and his self-respect. Once, a friend came across him in this deplorable state, lying on the road. So he got a sack and put him in feet first and put the sack on his shoulder and set off for home. On the way, another drunk appeared, reeling along, supported by a companion. At this, the man whose head hung out of the sack, woke up, and seeing the other in this pitiable state said reprovingly: 'Ah, unhappy man, in future drink two cups of wine less, then you will be able to walk as I do now—free and alone.'

Our own state is not different. We see faults because we do not love. If we had the least understanding of real love, the faults of those near to us would appear as good qualities.

THE LOVER AND HIS MISTRESS

A young man, brave and impetuous as a lion, was for five years in love with a woman. In one of the eyes of this beauty was a small speck, but the man, when gazing on the beauty of his mistress, never saw it. How could a man, so much in love, notice a tiny flaw? However, in time, his love began to dwindle and he regained his power over himself. It was then that he noticed the speck, and asked her how it had come about. She said: 'It appeared at the time when your love began to cool. When your love for me became defective my eye became so for you.'

O blind of heart! how long will you continue to look for the faults of others? Strive to be aware of those things you hide so carefully. When you see your faults in all their ugliness you will not bother so much about those of others.

THE POLICEMAN AND THE DRUNKEN MAN

A policeman knocked down a drunken man who said to him: 'Why get into such a passion? You are doing something illegal. I am harming no one, but you are mixing yourself up with drunkenness and throwing it into the road. You are much more drunk than I, but no one notices it. Then leave me alone, and ask for justice against yourself.'

36

QUESTION OF THE TWENTIETH BIRD

Another bird said to the Hoopoe: 'O Leader of the Way, what ought I to ask the Simurgh if I arrive at the place where he dwells? Since by him the world will be lighted up, I shall not know what to ask. If I knew what is the best thing to ask of the Simurgh on his throne, my mind would be easier.'

The Hoopoe replied: 'O Idiot! What! You don't know what to ask? Ask that which you wish most. A man should know what he wishes to ask, though the Simurgh himself is far better than anything you can wish. Will you learn from him what you wish to ask?'

PRAYER OF SHAIKH RŪBDAR

When Bu Alī Rūbdar was at the point of death he pronounced these words: 'My soul is on my lips in expectation of eternal welfare. The doors of heaven are open, and they have placed a throne for me in paradise. The saints who dwell in the palace of immortality cry with the voices of nightingales: "Enter, O true lover. Be thankful and walk with joy, for no one on earth has ever seen this place." O God, if I obtain thy grace and favour my soul will not slip from the hand of certainty. I shall not bow my head as in the world of men, for my soul has been formed through thy love, and thus I know neither heaven nor hell.

'If I am reduced to ashes there will not be found in me another being than Thou. I know Thee but I know not religion or unbelief. I am Thou, Thou art I. I desire Thee, my soul is in Thee. Thou alone art necessary to me. Thou art for me this world and the world to come. Satisfy, ever so little, the need of my wounded heart. Show, even a little, thy love for me, for I breathe only by Thee.'

WORDS OF GOD TO DAVID

God from on High said to David: 'Say to my servants: "O handful of earth! If I had not heaven for recompense and hell for punishment, would you ever think of me? If there were neither light nor fire, would you ever think of me? But since I merit supreme respect you must adore me without hope or fear; and yet, if you were never upheld by hope or fear would you ever think of me? Since I am your Lord, you should worship me from the depths of your heart. Reject all that which is not I, burn it to ashes and cast the ashes to the wind of excellence." '

MAHMŪD AND AYĀZ

One day, Mahmūd called his favourite to him and gave him his crown and made him sit on his throne, and said to him: 'Ayāz, I give you my kingdom and my army. Reign, for this country is yours; and I now wish you to take my place and throw your ear-ring of slavery to the Moon and the Fish.'

When the officers and courtiers heard about it their eyes went black from jealousy and they said: 'Never in the world has a king given so much honour to a slave.' But Ayāz wept, and they said to him: 'Have you lost your senses? You are no longer a slave but of the royalty. Why do you weep? Be contented!' Ayāz replied: 'You do not see things as they are, you do not understand that the Sultan of this great country has exiled me from his presence. He wishes me to rule his kingdom, but I do not wish to be separated from him. I wish to obey him but not to leave him. What have I to do with government and royalty? My happiness is in seeing his face.'

Learn from Ayāz how to serve God, you who remain idle day and night, occupied with cheap and vulgar pleasures. Ayāz descends from the summit of power, but you do not stir from where you are, neither have you any wish to change yourself. To whom will you at last be able to tell your sorrows? So long as you depend on paradise and hell, how will you be able to understand the secret which I wish to reveal to you; but when you no longer depend on those two the dawn of the mystery will lift itself from the night. The garden of paradise moreover is not for the indifferent; and the empyrean is only for the men of heart.

PRAYER OF RAB'IAH

'O God, you who know the secret of all things, bring to pass the worldly desires of my enemies, and grant my friends the eternity of the future life. But as for me, I am free of both. Even if I possessed this present world or the world of the future, I should esteem them little in comparison with being near to you. I need only you. If I should turn my eyes towards the two worlds, or desire anything but you, I should be no more than an unbeliever.'

WORDS OF GOD TO DAVID

The Creator of the World spoke to David from behind the veil of mystery. 'All that exists, whether good or bad, visible or invisible, moving or unmoving, is only a substitute if it is not myself, for whom you will find neither replacement nor equal. Since nothing can take the place of me, do not separate yourself from me. I am necessary to you, you are dependent on me. Therefore do not desire that which offers itself if it be not I.'

SULTAN MAHMŪD AND THE IDOL OF SOMNAT

Mahmūd and his army discovered at Somnat an idol named Lāt, which Mahmūd decided to destroy. The Hindus, to save it, offered ten times its weight in gold, but Mahmūd refused and ordered a great fire to be made to burn the idol. Then one of his officers permitted himself to say: 'Would it not be better, Sire, to accept the gold and not to burn the idol?' 'I should think,' said Mahmūd, 'that on the day of supreme reckoning the Creator would say to the assembled universe: "Listen to what Azaz and Mahmūd have done—the first fashioned idols, the second sold them!"'

They say that when the idol of the fire-worshippers was burning a hundred maunds of precious stones fell out, so Mahmūd obtained treasure as well. He said: 'Lāt has got what he deserved and God has rewarded me.'

ANOTHER ANECDOTE OF MAHMŪD

When this torch of kings left Gaznā to make war on the Hindus and encountered their mighty army, he was cast down, and he made a vow to the King of Justice that if he were victorious he would give all the booty that fell into his hands to the dervishes. He gained the victory, and his army collected an enormous amount of treasure. When the black-faces had retreated leaving the plunder, Mahmūd said:

'Send this to the dervishes, for I have promised God to do
so, and I must keep my vow.' Then his officers protested
and said: 'Why give so much silver and gold to a handful
of men who do not fight! Why not give it to the army which
has borne the brunt of the battle, or, at least, put it in the
treasury?'

The Sultan hesitated between his vow and the protests
of his army. Meanwhile, Bu Hassein, an idiot of God, who
was intelligent but uneducated, passed along that way.
Mahmūd seeing him in the distance said: 'Call that idiot;
tell him to come here and say what ought to be done, and I
will act accordingly; since he fears neither the Sultan nor
the army he will give an impartial opinion.' When the
Sultan had put the case to Bu Hassein, the latter said: 'Sire,
it is a question of two obols, but if you wish to act becomingly
towards God, think no more, O my dear, about these two
obols; and if you win another victory by his grace, be
ashamed to hold back two obols. Since God has given you
the victory, can that which belongs to God belong to you?'

Mahmūd thereupon gave the treasure to the dervishes,
and became a great monarch.

37

QUESTION OF THE TWENTY-FIRST BIRD

Another bird said to the Hoopoe: 'Tell us, O you who wish
to lead us to the unknown Majesty, what is most appreciated
at that court? It is necessary when going to kings to bear
precious gifts; only vile men approach them with empty
hands.'

The Hoopoe replied: 'If you follow my advice you will
take to the country of the Simurgh what is not found there.
Is it fitting that one should take what is there already? True
knowledge is found there, secrets are found there, obedience

to higher beings is found there. Take then the ardour of love and the longing of the spirit; no one can offer other than this. If a single sigh of love goes to that place it will carry the perfume of the heart. That place is consecrated to the essence of the soul. If a man should heave one sigh of true contrition he will forthwith be in possession of salvation.'

JOSEPH AND ZULAIKHA

At the time when Zulaikha was enjoying her high rank and dignity she had Joseph put in prison, and told one of her slaves to give him fifty blows with a stick. 'Strike him hard,' she said, 'so that I shall be able to hear his cries.' But this good man did not wish to hurt Joseph, so he took the skin of an animal, and said: 'When I beat it, cry out at each stroke.' When Zulaikha heard the cries she went to the cell and said: 'You are too easy with him, strike harder.' Then the slave said to Joseph, 'O radiance of the sun! If Zulaikha examines you and does not see any marks, she will punish me severely. Now, uncover your shoulders and brace up your heart and bear the blows. If you cry out from the blows she will take less notice of the marks.' Joseph uncovered his shoulders, the stick fell, and his cries went up to heaven. When Zulaikha heard him she went and said: 'It is enough, these cries have produced their effect. Before, his groans were nothing; now, they are very real.'

THE SHAIKH BEN ALI TŪCI

Ben Ali Tūci, one of the great sages of his time, walked in the valley of awareness and attention. I do not know of anyone who possessed such grace and who attained such perfection. He once said: 'In the other world, the unfortunate damned will see clearly the dwellers in heaven, who will be able to tell them about the joys of that place and the taste of union. The fortunate will say: "Vulgar joys do not exist here, because the sun of divine beauty has appeared to us, and it is such that the eight paradises appear to be dark. In the brightness of this beauty there remains of eternity neither name nor trace!" Then those in the underworld will say: "We sense that what you say is true, but for us in this horrible place it is evident that we have incurred the anger of God, and for this we have been put far from his face. We are reminded of the fire of the underworld by the fire of remorse in our hearts." '

Strive to bear sorrow, affliction and wounds, and thereby show your zeal. If you are wounded, accept it, and do not give way to self-pity.

REQUEST TO MUHAMMAD

A man humbly asked permission to say a prayer on the carpet of the Prophet, who refused, and said: 'The earth and the sand are burning. Put your face on the burning sand and on the earth of the road, since all those who are wounded by love must have the imprint on their face, and the scar must be seen. Let the scar of the heart be seen, for by their scars are known the men who are in the way of love.'

38

QUESTION OF THE TWENTY-SECOND BIRD AND
THE DESCRIPTION OF THE FIRST VALLEY
OR
THE VALLEY OF THE QUEST

This bird said to the Hoopoe: 'O you who know the road of which you have told us and on which you wish us to accompany you, to me the way is dark, and in the gloom it appears to be very difficult, and many parasangs in length.'

The Hoopoe replied: 'We have seven valleys to cross and only after we have crossed them shall we discover the Simurgh. No one has ever come back into the world who

has made this journey, and it is impossible to say how many
parasangs there are in front of us. Be patient, O fearful one,
since all those who went by this road were in your state.

'The first valley is the Valley of the Quest, the second
the Valley of Love, the third is the Valley of Understanding,
the fourth is the Valley of Independence and Detachment,
the fifth of Pure Unity, the sixth is the Valley of Astonishment, and the seventh is the Valley of Poverty and Nothingness beyond which one can go no farther.

'When you enter the first valley, the Valley of the Quest,
a hundred difficulties will assail you; you will undergo a
hundred trials. There, the parrot of heaven is no more than
a fly. You will have to spend several years there, you will
have to make great efforts, and to change your state. You
will have to give up all that has seemed precious to you and
regard as nothing all that you possess. When you are sure
that you possess nothing, you will still have to detach yourself from all that exists. Your heart will then be saved from
perdition and you will see the pure light of Divine Majesty
and your real wishes will be multiplied to infinity. One who
enters here will be filled with such longing that he will give
himself up completely to the quest symbolized by this valley.
He will ask of his cup-bearer a draught of wine, and when he
has drunk it nothing else will matter except the pursuit of
his true aim. Then he will no longer fear the dragons, the
guardians of the door, which seek to devour him. When the
door is opened and he enters, then dogma, belief and
unbelief—all cease to exist.'

EXTRACT FROM GANJ-NĀMA THE BOOK OF
TREASURE OF OSMĀN AMRŪ

When God breathed the pure breath of life into the body
of Adam, which was only earth and water, he wished that
the hosts of angels should not know about it, and not even
suspect it. So he said to them: 'Prostrate yourselves before

Adam, O Celestial Spirits!' All of them then bowed themselves down on the earth, and when they were bowed down, God breathed the breath of life into Adam and none of them was aware of the secret that God wished to hide. That is, none but Iblis, who said to himself, 'No one shall see me bend the knee. Even if my head falls from my body, it will not be as bad as doing what God wishes. I know very well that it is not just a question of Adam being on the earth, so I don't intend to bow my head down and not see the secret.' So instead of bowing down, Iblis watched, and saw the secret. Afterwards God said: 'O you who were lying in wait, you have stolen my secret, and for this I shall bring about your death, for I do not wish any other being to know about it. When an earthly king hides treasure he kills the person who saw it being hid. You are this person.'

'Lord,' said Iblis, 'grant a respite, for I am your servant; and tell me how I can expiate my sin?' 'Since you ask,' said God, 'I will grant you a respite; nevertheless, from this moment I shall put on your neck the collar of malediction and I impose on you the name of liar and slanderer, so that everyone will be on guard against you until the day of resurrection.'

Iblis said: 'What have I to fear from your malediction since this pure treasure has been manifested to me? If malediction comes from you so does mercy. Where there is poison there is also an antidote. You curse some creatures and bless others. Now that I have transgressed I am the creature of your malediction.'

If you cannot discover and understand the secret of which I speak, it is not because it does not exist but because you do not seek rightly. If you make a distinction between the things which come from God you are not a man on the path of the spirit. If you consider yourself honoured by the diamond and humiliated by the stone, God is not with you. Note well, you should not love the diamond and detest the stone, for both come from God. If your mistress in a moment of frenzy throws a stone at you, that is better than a jewel from another woman.

On the way of self-perfection a man must not loiter for an instant. If he should stop for a moment working on himself he will slip back.

STORY OF MAJNŪN

A man who loved God saw Majnūn sifting the earth of the road and said: 'Majnūn, what are you looking for?' 'I am looking for Laïla,' he said. The man asked: 'Do you hope to find Laïla there?' 'I look for her everywhere,' said Majnūn, 'in the hope of finding her somewhere.'

YŪSSUF HAMDANĪ

Yūssuf Hamdanī was a celebrated man of his time, a seer, who understood the secrets of the worlds. He said: 'All that which is seen, either on the heights or in the depths—each atom in fact, is another Jacob asking for news of Joseph whom he has lost.'

In the spiritual way both love and hope are necessary. If you do not have these you had better give up the quest. Man must try to be patient. But is a lover ever patient? Be patient and strive with hope to find someone who will show you the way. Keep yourself within yourself and do not let exterior life capture you.

STORY OF ABŪ SA'ID MAHNAH

Shaikh Mahnah was in a state of great perplexity, his heart broken in two, when he saw in the distance an old villager of pious appearance, walking leisurely, while from his body emanated a bright light. The shaikh saluted him and then told him about the sad state he was in. The old villager listened, and after thinking a little said: 'O Bu Sa'id, if they were to fill with millet, not once but a hundred times, the space from lowest earth to the throne of God, and if a bird took one grain of millet in a thousand years, and then flew a hundred times round the world, even in all that time your soul would have no news of the celestial court and Bu Sa'id would still be far off.'

Great patience is necessary for those who suffer; but no one is patient. When the quest is diverted from the inner to the outer, even if it should extend over the universe, in the end it will be unsatisfying. He who is not engaged in the quest of the inner life is no more than an animal—what shall I say? He does not even exist, he is a non-entity, a form without a soul.

MAHMŪD AND THE SEEKER AFTER GOLD

One night Mahmūd, riding alone, saw a man sifting earth for gold; his head was bent and he had piled up here and there heaps of sifted dust. The sultan looked at him and then threw his bracelet among the heaps and rode off like the wind. The following night Mahmūd returned and found the man still sifting. 'What you found yesterday,' said the sultan, 'should be enough to pay the tribute of the world, and yet you still continue to sift!' The man replied: 'I found the bracelet you threw down, and it is because I have found such a treasure that I must continue to search as long as I live.'

Be like this man and search until the door is opened to you. Your eyes will not be always shut; seek the door.

A SENTENCE OF RĀBI'AH

A man prayed: 'O Lord, open a door that I may come to you.' Rābi'ah, hearing him, said: 'O idiot! is the door shut?'

39

THE SECOND VALLEY
OR
THE VALLEY OF LOVE

The Hoopoe continued: 'The next valley is The Valley of Love. To enter it one must be a flaming fire—what shall I say? A man must himself be fire. The face of the lover must be enflamed, burning and impetuous as fire. True love knows no after-thoughts; with love, good and evil cease to exist.

'But as for you, the heedless and the careless, this discourse will not touch you, your teeth will not even nibble at it. A loyal person stakes ready money, stakes his head even, to be united to his friend. Others content themselves with promising what they will do for you tomorrow. If he who sets out on this way will not engage himself wholly and completely he will never be free from the sadness and melancholy which weigh him down. Until the falcon reaches his aim he is agitated and distressed. If a fish is thrown on to the beach by the waves it struggles to get back into the water.

'In this valley, love is represented by fire, and reason by smoke. When love comes reason disappears. Reason cannot live with the folly of love; love has nothing to do with human reason. If you possessed inner sight, the atoms of the visible world would be manifested to you. But if you look at things with the eye of ordinary reason you will never understand how necessary it is to love. Only a man who has been tested and is free can feel this. He who undertakes this journey should have a thousand hearts so that he can sacrifice one at every moment.'

AN AMOROUS KHOJA

A Khoja sold all that he possessed—furniture, slaves, and everything, to buy beer from a young beer-seller. He became

completely mad for love of this beer-seller. He was always
hungry because if he were given bread he sold it to buy beer.
At last someone asked him: 'What is this love that brings
you into such a pitiable state? Tell me the secret!' 'Love is
such,' he replied, 'that you will sell the merchandise of a
hundred worlds to buy beer. So long as you do not understand this, you will never experience the true feeling of love.'

A STORY OF MAJNUN

The parents of Laïla refused to let Majnūn go near their tents.
But Majnun, intoxicated with love, borrowed the skin of
a sheep from a shepherd in the desert, where Laïla's tribe
pitched their tents. He bent his head down and put on the
sheep-skin, and said to the shepherd: 'In the name of God,
let me crawl along in the middle of your sheep, then lead
the flock past Laïla's tent, so that I may perhaps discover
her sweet perfume, and being concealed in this skin may
contrive something.' The shepherd did as Majnūn wished,
and as they passed her tent he saw her, and swooned away.
The shepherd then carried him from the tents into the
desert and threw water on his face to cool his burning
love.

Another day, Majnūn was with some companions in the
desert, and one of them asked him: 'How can you, a noble-
man, go about naked? I will get some clothes for you if you
wish.' Majnūn said: 'No garments that I can wear are worthy
of my friend, so for me there is nothing better than my bare
body or a sheepskin. She, for me, is as ispand to avert the
evil eye. Majnūn would willingly wear garments of silk and
cloth of gold, but he prefers this sheepskin by means of
which he caught sight of Laïla.'

Love should tear aside your prudence. Love changes
your attitude. To love is to give up your ordinary life and
forsake your tawdry pleasures.

A BEGGAR IN LOVE WITH AYĀZ

A poor dervish once fell in love with Ayāz, and the news soon spread. When Ayāz rode through the street, perfumed with musk, this spiritual wanton would wait and run out to see him, and would stare at him as a polo player fixes his eye on the ball. At last they told Mahmūd about this beggar being in love with Ayāz. One day, when Ayāz was riding with the sultan, the latter stopped and looked at this dervish and he saw that the soul of Ayāz was as a grain of barley and the face of the man as a ball of dough which encloses it.

He saw that the back of the beggar was curved like a mallet, and his head was turning every way at once like the ball in polo. Mahmūd said: 'Miserable beggar, do you expect to drink from the same cup as the Sultan?' 'Although you call me a beggar,' replied the dervish, 'I am not inferior to you in the play of love. Love and poverty go together. You are the sovereign, and your heart is luminous; but for love, a burning heart like mine is necessary. Your love is commonplace. I suffer from the pain of absence. You are with the beloved; but in love one must know how to endure the pain of absence.' The sultan said: 'O you who have withdrawn from ordinary existence, love to you is as a game of polo?' 'It is,' replied the beggar, 'because the ball is always in movement, as I am, and I as the ball. The ball and I have heads that turn, though we have neither hands nor feet. We can speak together about the suffering that the mallet causes us; but the ball is happier than I, for the pony touches it from time to time with its feet. The ball receives the blows of the mallet on his body, but I feel them in my heart.'

'Poor Dervish!' said the sultan, 'you boast of your poverty, but where is your evidence?'

'If I sacrifice everything for love,' replied the dervish, 'that is a token of my spiritual poverty. And if you, O Mahmūd, ever have the experience of real love, sacrifice your life for it; if not you have no right to speak of love.'

So saying, he died, and the world became dark for Mahmūd.

AN ARAB IN PERSIA

An Arab once went to Persia and was astonished at the customs of the country. One day he happened to pass the dwelling of a group of Qalandars and saw a handful of men who said not a word. They had no wives, and not even an obol, but they were pure of heart and undefiled. Each held a flask of muddy wine which he carefully filled before sitting down. The Arab felt sympathetic towards these men; he stopped and at that moment his mind and heart fell on to the road.

At this the Qalandars said: 'Enter, O man of nothing!' So he went in, willy-nilly, just like that! He was given a cup of wine and at once lost his senses. He became drunk and his strength was reduced to nothing. His gold and silver and valuables were taken from him by one of the Qalandars, more wine was given to him and at last they put him out of the house. Then this Arab returned to his own country, one-eyed and poor, his state changed and his lips dry. When he arrived at his native place his companions asked him: 'What is the matter? What have you done with your money and valuables? Were they stolen while you slept? Have you done badly in Persia? Tell us! Perhaps we can help you!'

'I was moving about in the street,' said he, 'and all at once I fell in with the Qalandars. I know nothing else except that my possessions and I were parted and now I have nothing.' They asked him to describe the Qalandars. He only replied, 'They simply said to me "Enter"'.

The Arab remained ever after in a state of surprise and astonishment, like a child, and dumbfounded by the word 'Enter'.

You too, put your foot forward. If you do not wish to, then follow your fantasies. But if you prefer the secrets of the love of your soul you will sacrifice everything. You will lose what you considered to be valuable, but you will soon hear the sacramental word 'Enter'.

THE LOVER WHO LOST HIS MISTRESS

A man of high ideals fell in love with a beautiful young woman. But, as time went on, she to whom he had given his heart became thin, and as yellow as a sprig of saffron. The bright day faded from her heart; and death, who was watching from far off, came near. When her lover learnt of this he took a dagger and said: 'I will go and kill my mistress where she lies so that this beauty, who is like a wonderful picture, does not die by nature.' They said to him: 'Are you mad! Why do you wish to kill her when she is already at the point of death?' The lover said: 'If she dies at my hands they will kill me, since I am forbidden to do that myself. Then, on the day of resurrection, we shall be together as we are now. If I am put to death because of my passion for her we shall be as one, as the clear flame of a lighted candle.'

Lovers who have staked their lives for their love have entered on the Path. In the life of the Spirit they are united to the object of their affection.

ABRAHAM AND THE ANGEL OF DEATH

When the friend of God came to die he was reluctant to deliver his soul to Azrael. 'Wait,' he said to Azrael. 'Has the King of the Universe asked for it?' But God, The Most High, said to Abraham: 'If you truly were my friend, would you not wish to come to me? He who regrets giving his life for his friend shall have it torn from him with a sword.' Then, one of those present said: 'O Abraham, Light of the World, why will you not give up your life with good grace to Azrael? Lovers in the Spiritual Way stake their lives for their love; you set store on yours.' Abraham said: 'How can

I let go my life when Azrael has put his foot in the way? I
disregarded his request because I thought only of God.
When Nimrod cast me into the fire and Gabriel came to me,
I disregarded him because I thought only of God. Seeing
that I turned my head from Gabriel, can I be expected to
give up my soul to Azrael? When I hear God say, "Give me
your life!" then it will be worth no more than a grain of
barley. How can I give my life to someone unless he asks
for it? That is all I have to say.'

40

THE THIRD VALLEY
OR
THE VALLEY OF UNDERSTANDING

The Hoopoe continued: 'After the valley of which I have
spoken, there comes another—The Valley of Understanding,
which has neither beginning nor end. No way is equal to
this way, and the distance to be travelled to cross it is beyond
reckoning.

'Understanding, for each traveller, is enduring; but knowledge is temporary. The soul, like the body, is in a state of
progress or decline; and the Spiritual Way reveals itself only
in the degree to which the traveller has overcome his faults
and weaknesses, his sleep and his inertia, and each will
approach nearer to his aim according to his effort. Even if
a gnat were to fly with all its might could it equal the speed
of the wind? There are different ways of crossing this Valley,
and all birds do not fly alike. Understanding can be arrived
at variously—some have found the Mihrāb, others the idol.
When the sun of understanding brightens this road each receives light according to his merit and he finds the degree
assigned to him in the understanding of truth. When the
mystery of the essence of beings reveals itself clearly to him

the furnace of this world becomes a garden of flowers. He who is striving will be able to see the almond in its hard shell. He will no longer be pre-occupied with himself, but will look up at the face of his friend. In each atom he will see the whole; he will ponder over thousands of bright secrets.

'But, how many have lost their way in this search for one who has found the mysteries! It is necessary to have a deep and lasting wish to become as we ought to be in order to cross this difficult valley. Once you have tasted the secrets you will have a real wish to understand them. But, whatever you may attain, never forget the words of the Koran, "Is there anything more?"

'As for you who are asleep (and I cannot commend you for this), why not put on mourning? You, who have not seen the beauty of your friend, get up and search! How long will you stay as you are, like a donkey without a halter!'

TEARS OF STONE

There is a man in China who gathers stones, without ceasing. He sheds abundant tears, and as the tears fall on the ground they change into stones, which again he gathers. If the clouds were to weep tears like these it would be a matter for sorrow and sighing.

Real knowledge becomes the possession of the true seeker. If it is necessary to seek knowledge in China, then go. But knowledge is distorted by the formal mind, it becomes petrified, like stones. How long must real knowledge continue to be misunderstood? This world, this house of sorrows, is in darkness; but true knowledge is a jewel, it will burn like a lamp and guide you in this gloomy place. If you spurn this jewel you will ever be a prey to regret. If you lag behind you will weep bitter tears. But if you sleep little by night, and fast by day, you may find what you seek. Seek, then, and be lost in the quest.

THE SLEEPING LOVER

A lover, uneasy, troubled in his mind, and worn out with sighing, fell asleep on the mound of a grave. His mistress coming upon him and finding him asleep wrote a note and pinned it to his cloak. When he woke and read what she had written he groaned with anguish, for it said: 'O dumb man! rise up, and if you are a merchant, do business and get money; if you are an ascetic, wake at night and pray to God and be his slave. But if you are a lover, be ashamed of yourself. What has sleep to do with a lover's eyes? By day he measures the wind; at night his burning heart lights up his face with the brightness of the moon. As you are no such man, no longer boast of loving me. If a man can sleep elsewhere than in his shroud I may call him a lover—but, of himself.'

THE SENTINEL IN LOVE

A soldier was in love. Even if not on guard he could never rest. At last, a friend begged him to have a few hours' sleep. The soldier said: 'I am a sentinel, and I am in love. How can I rest? A soldier on duty must not sleep, so it is an advantage to him to be in love. Each night love puts me to the test, and thus I can stay awake and keep watch on the fort. This love is a friend to the sentinel, for wakefulness becomes part of him; he who reaches this state will ever be on the watch.'

Do not sleep, O man, if you are striving for knowledge of yourself. Guard well the fortress of your heart, for there are thieves everywhere. Do not let brigands steal the jewel you carry. True knowledge will come to him who can stay awake. He who patiently keeps watch will be aware when God comes near him. True lovers who wish to surrender themselves to the intoxication of love go apart together. He who has spiritual love holds in his hand the keys of the two worlds. If one is a woman one becomes a man; and if one is a man one becomes a deep ocean.

MAHMŪD AND THE IDIOT OF GOD

One day, in the desert, Mahmūd saw a faquir whose head
was bowed in sadness and whose back was bent with sorrow.
When the sultan went up to him the man said: 'Begone! or
I will give you a hundred blows. Go away, I tell you, you are
no monarch but a man of vile thinking, an unbeliever in the
grace of God.' Mahmūd answered sharply: 'Speak to me as
befits a sultan, not in that fashion.' The faquir replied:
'If you knew, O ignorant one, how you are turned upside
down, earth and ashes would not suffice; you would lament
without ceasing and put fire on your head.'

41

THE FOURTH VALLEY
OR
THE VALLEY OF
INDEPENDENCE AND DETACHMENT

The Hoopoe continued: 'Then comes the valley where there
is neither the desire to possess nor the wish to discover. In
this state of the soul a cold wind blows, so violent that in a
moment it devastates an immense space: the seven oceans
are no more than a pool, the seven planets a mere spark, the
seven heavens a corpse, the seven hells broken ice. Then, an
astonishing thing, beyond reason! An ant has the strength of
a hundred elephants, and a hundred caravans perish while a
rook is filling his crop.

'In order that Adam might receive the celestial light, hosts
of green-clad angels were consumed by sorrow. So that
Noah might become a carpenter of God and build the ark,
thousands of creatures perished in the waters. Myriads of
gnats fell on the army of Abrahah so that that king would be
overthrown. Thousands of the first-born died so that Moses
might see God. Thousands of people took the Christian

girdle so that Christ could possess the secret of God. Thousands of hearts and souls were pillaged so that Muhammad might ascend for one night to heaven. In this Valley nothing old or new has value; you can act or not act. If you saw a whole world burning until hearts were only shish kabab, it would be only a dream compared to reality. If myriads of souls were to fall into this boundless ocean it would be as a drop of dew. If heaven and earth were to burst into minute particles it would be no more than a leaf falling from a tree; and if everything were to be annihilated, from the fish to the moon, would there be found in the depths of a pit the leg of a lame ant? If there remain no trace of either of men or jinn, the secret of a drop of water from which all has been formed is still to be pondered over.'

THE YOUNG MAN FALLEN INTO A PIT

In my village there was a young man beautiful as Joseph, who fell into a pit and the earth caved in on him. When they got him out he was in a sad state. This excellent young man was called Mūhammad, and was liked by everyone. His father groaned when he saw him and said: 'O Mūhammad, you are the light of my eyes and the soul of your father. O my son, say one word to your father!' The son said one word and gave up the ghost, and that is all.

O you who are a young pupil on the path of spiritual knowledge and who are able to observe and ponder, think about Mūhammad and Adam; think about Adam and the atoms, the whole and the particles of the whole; speak of the earth and heavens, of the mountains and the ocean; speak of the fairies and the gods, of men and angels, of a hundred thousand pure souls; speak of the painful moment of the giving up of the soul; say that every individual, soul and body, are nothing. If you reduce the two worlds to dust and sift them a hundred times, what will it be for you? It will be like a palace upside down, and you will find nothing on the surface of the siftings.

This Valley is not so easy to cross as you in your simplicity perhaps think. Even when the blood of your heart shall fill the ocean, you will only be able to make the first stage. Even if you were to journey over all the ways of the world you would still find yourself at the first step. No traveller has seen the limit of this journey neither has he found a remedy for love. If you halt you are petrified, or you may even die; if you continue on your way, always advancing, you will hear until eternity the cry: 'Go still further.' You can neither go nor stay. It is no advantage either to live or to die.

What profit have you derived from all that has befallen you? What have you gained from the difficulties you have been able to endure? It matters little whether you beat your head or no. O you who hear me, remain silent, and work actively.

Give up your useless aims and pursue the essential things. Be occupied as little as possible with things of the outer world but much with things of the inner world; then right action will overcome inaction. But those who find no remedy in acting, had better do nothing since you must know when to act and when to refrain from action. But how to know what you cannot know? And yet it is possible to act as you should, even without knowing. Forget all that you have done up till now, and strive to be independent and sufficient in yourself, though sometimes you will weep and sometimes rejoice. In this Fourth Valley the lightning of power, which is the discovery of your own resources, of self-sufficiency, blazes up so that the heat consumes a hundred worlds. Since hundreds of worlds are reduced to powder is it strange that yours also will disappear?

THE ASTROLOGER

Have you ever seen a wise man set out a tablet and cover it with sand? There he traces figures and designs, and places the stars and planets, the heavens and the earth. Sometimes he makes a prediction from the heavens, sometimes from earth. He also draws the constellations and the signs of the Zodiac and indicates the rising and setting of the stars, and from this he deduces good or bad auguries. When he has cast a horoscope, of good or bad fortune, he takes the tablet by a corner and scatters the sand, and it is as if all those signs and figures had never existed.

The accidental surface of this world is like the tablet. If you have not the strength to resist the longing for the superficial things of this world turn away from it and sit in a corner. Men and women come into life without any idea of the inner and the outer worlds.

THE FLY AND THE HONEY

A fly in search of honey saw a beehive in a garden. The desire for honey put her into such a state that you would have taken her for an Azad, and she called out: 'I will give an obol to anyone who will help me get into this hive.' Someone took pity on her, and for an obol helped her in. But no sooner was she in than her legs became stuck in the honey. Though she fluttered her wings and skipped about it became worse, and she moaned: 'This is tyranny, this is poison. I am caught. I gave an obol to get in but would gladly give two to get out.'

'In this Valley,' continued the Hoopoe, 'no one must remain inactive, and one must enter it only after having reached a certain stage of development. Now it is time to work instead of living in uncertainty and passing one's time heedlessly. Rouse yourself from apathy, renounce inner and outer attachments, and cross this difficult valley; for if you do not renounce them you will become more heedless than the worshippers of many gods, and you will never become self-sufficient.'

WORDS OF A SHAIKH TO A PUPIL

A pupil demanded an answer from his master to an idle question. The shaikh said: 'First wash your face. Can the perfume of musk be smelled in the odour of putrefaction? I do not impart knowledge to drunken men.'

A DERVISH IN LOVE WITH THE DOG-KEEPER'S DAUGHTER

There was once a celebrated shaikh who wore the khirka of poverty, but he fell deeply in love with the daughter of a man who looked after dogs, and in hope of seeing her lived and slept in the street. The girl's mother discovered this, and said to the shaikh: 'You know, of course, that we are dog-keepers, but since you have lost your heart to our daughter you may marry her in a year, and lodge with us; and you must consent to be a dog-keeper and accept our way of life.' As the shaikh was no weakling in love he took off his Sufi mantle and set to work. Every day he took a dog into the bazaar, and continued to do so for almost a year. One day, another Sufi, who was also his friend, said to him: 'O man of nothing, for thirty years you have worked in, and pondered over, spiritual things, and now you do what your equals have never done!' The shaikh replied: 'You do not see things in their true light, so stop protesting. If you wish to understand, learn that God alone knows the secret and only he can reveal it. It is better to appear ridiculous than, like you, never to have penetrated the secrets of the spiritual Way.'

42

THE FIFTH VALLEY
OR
THE VALLEY OF UNITY

The Hoopoe continued: 'You will next have to cross the Valley of Unity. In this valley everything is broken in pieces and then unified. All who raise their heads here raise them from the same collar. Although you seem to see many beings, in reality there is only one—all make one which is complete in its unity. Again, that which you see as a unity is not different from that which appears as number. And as the Being of whom I speak is beyond unity and numbering, cease to think of eternity as before and after, and since these two eternities have vanished, cease to speak of them. When all that is visible is reduced to nothing, what is there left to contemplate?'

REPLY OF AN IDIOT OF GOD

Someone asked a man of understanding: 'What is the world? What can it be compared to?' He replied: 'This world, which is compounded of horrors and crime, is like a palm-tree of wax, adorned with a hundred colours. If you squeeze the tree it becomes a lump of wax; therefore the colours and shapes you admire are not worth an obol. If there is unity there cannot be duality; neither "I" nor "Thou" has significance.

'But what is the use of my words, though they come from the depth of my soul, if you do not ponder over them. If you have fallen into the ocean of exterior life, like a partridge whose wings and feathers cannot support it, then never cease to think about how to reach the shore.'

SHAIKH BŪ ALĪ DAKKAH

An old woman offered Bū Alī a piece of gold saying: 'Accept this from me.' He replied: 'I can accept things only from God.' The old woman retorted: 'Where did you learn to see double? You are not a man of power to bind and unbind. If you were not squint-eyed would you see several things at once?'

There is neither Ka'aba nor Pagoda. Learn from my mouth the true doctrine—the eternal existence of Being. We must not see anyone other than Him. We are in Him, by Him, and with Him. We may also be outside these states. Whoever is not immersed in the Ocean of Unity is not worthy of the race of men.

The day will come when the Sun will draw aside the veil which covers it. So long as you are separate, good and evil will arise in you, but when you lose yourself in the sun of the divine essence they will be transcended by love. While you loiter on the road you will be held back by faults and weaknesses. Have you not yet realized that in your body there are conceit, vanity, self-pride, self-love and other dirty things! Though the serpent and the scorpion may seem to be dead within you they are only asleep; and if something touches them they will wake up with the strength of a hundred dragons. In each of us is a Hell of serpents. If you make yourself secure against these unclean creatures you may remain tranquil; if not, they will sting you even in the dust of the tomb until the day of reckoning.

And now, O Attar, leave your metaphorical discourses and return to the description of the mysterious Valley of Unity.

The Hoopoe continued: 'When the spiritual traveller enters this valley he will disappear and be lost to sight because the Unique Being will manifest himself; he will be silent because this Being will speak.

'The part will become the whole, or rather, there will be neither part nor whole. In the School of the Secret you will see thousands of men with intellectual knowledge, their lips parted in silence. What is intellectual knowledge here? It stops on the threshold of the door like a blind child. He who discovers something of this secret turns his face from the kingdom of the two worlds. The Being I speak of does not exist separately; everyone is this Being, existence and non-existence is this Being.'

PRAYER OF LOKMĀN SARKHASĪ

Lokmān of Sarkhasī said: 'O God, I am old, and my mind is troubled; I have strayed from the Way. To an old slave they give a certificate of freedom. In your service, O my King, my black hair has become white as snow. I am a slave, cast down; give me now the certificate of freedom.'

A voice from the inner world replied: 'You, who have been specially admitted to the sanctuary, know that he who wishes for release from slavery must discard his reason, and not occupy himself with cares and anxieties.'

Lokmān said: 'O my God, I desire only you, and I know that I must not give way to imagination or care and anxiety.' When Lokmān had renounced these things, he said: 'Now I do not know what I am. I am not a slave, but what am I? My slavery is ended, but my freedom has not taken place: in my heart is neither joy nor sadness. I am without quality, yet I am not deprived of it. I am a contemplative, yet I do not possess contemplation. I do not know if Thou art I or I am Thou; I have been reduced to nothing in Thee and duality has been lost.'

A LOVER RESCUES HIS MISTRESS
FROM THE WATER

A young woman fell into a river, and her lover jumped in to save her. When he reached her she said: 'Oh, why do you risk your life because of me?' He said, 'For me there exists no other person than you. When we are together then truly I am you and you are me. We two are one. Our two bodies are one, and that is all.'

When duality disappears, unity is found.

ANOTHER STORY OF MAHMŪD AND AYĀZ

It is related that once Farouk and Masoud were present at a review of Mahmūd's army, which consisted of innumerable elephants, horses and troops, so that the earth was as though covered with ants and locusts. Ayāz and Hassan accompanied Mahmūd who was seated on a high place.

As the immense army marched past them the great monarch unloosed his tongue and said to Ayāz: 'My son, all these elephants and horses and men of mine are now yours, for my love for you is such that I look on you as king.' Although these words were said by the renowned Mahmūd, Ayāz appeared indifferent and unmoved; he neither thanked the king nor commented. Hassan, astonished, said to him: 'Ayāz, a King has honoured you, a simple slave, and you show not the least sign of gratitude; you neither bow nor prostrate yourself in token of respect.' Ayāz thought a little and then said: 'I must give two answers to your reproach: the first is that if I, who have neither stability nor position, wish to show my devotion to the King, I can only fall in the dust before him in a sort of humiliation or else sing his praises in a whining voice. Between doing too much or too little it is better to do nothing. The slave is the King's, and his respect for the King is taken for granted. As for the honour this fortunate monarch has done me, if the two worlds should proclaim his praises their testimony would not be equal to his merit. If I do not behave ostentatiously and protest my fidelity it is because I feel I am not worthy to do so.'

Hassan said: 'O Ayāz, I see now that you are grateful, and I give you credit for being worthy of a hundred favours.' Then he added, 'Now give me the second answer.' But Ayāz said, 'I cannot speak freely before you, I can only do so if I am alone with the King. You are not Mahrām of the secret.' So the king asked Hassan to leave them, and when there was neither 'we' nor 'I' Ayāz said: 'When the King deigns to cast his eyes on me he annihilates my existence by the brightness of his rays. Since in the light of his glorious

sun I no longer exist, how shall I prostrate myself? Ayāz is
his shadow, lost in the sun of his face.'

43

THE SIXTH VALLEY
THE VALLEY OF ASTONISHMENT
AND BEWILDERMENT

After the Valley of Unity comes the Valley of Astonishment
and Bewilderment, where one is a prey to sadness and dejection. There sighs are like swords, and each breath a bitter
sigh; there, is sorrow and lamentation, and a burning eagerness. It is at once day and night. There, is fire, yet a man is
depressed and despondent. How, in his bewilderment, shall
he continue his way? But he who has achieved unity forgets
all and forgets himself. If he is asked: 'Are you, or are you
not? Have you or have you not the feeling of existence? Are
you in the middle or on the border? Are you mortal or
immortal?' he will reply with certainty: 'I know nothing, I
understand nothing, I am unaware of myself. I am in love,
but with whom I do not know. My heart is at the same time
both full and empty of love.'

THE PRINCESS IN LOVE WITH HER SLAVE

A king, whose empire stretched to the far horizons, had a
daughter as beautiful as the moon. Before her loveliness even
the fairies were abashed. Her dimpled chin resembled the
well of Joseph, and the locks of her hair wounded a hundred
hearts. Her eyebrows were twin bows, and when she loosed
their arrows the space between sang her praise. Her eyes,
languorous as the narcissus, threw thorns of her eyelashes in
the path of the wise. Her face was as the sun when he took
the moon's virginity. The Angel Gabriel could not tear his
eyes from the pearls and rubies of her mouth. A smile of her

lips dried up the water of life in the beholder, who yet begged alms from these same lips. Whoever glanced at her chin fell headlong into a spring of bubbling water.

The king also had a slave, a youth, so handsome that the sun grew pale and the light of the moon diminished. When he walked in the streets and market-place crowds stopped to gaze at him.

By chance one day the princess saw this slave, and in a moment her heart slipped from her hand. Reason forsook her and love took possession. Her soul, sweet as Shīrīn, turned bitter. Withdrawing from her companions she mused, and musing and reflecting, began to burn. Then she called her ten young maids of honour. They were excellent musicians and played on the shawms and pipes; their voices were those of nightingales, and their singing, which tore the soul, was worthy of David. Gathering them around her she told them about her state, saying that she was ready to sacrifice her name, her honour, and her life for the love of this youth; for when one is deep in love one is good for nothing else. 'But,' she said, 'if I tell him of my love no doubt he will do something rash. If it becomes known that I have been intimate with a slave both he and I will suffer. On the other hand, if he does not possess me, I shall die lamenting behind the curtain of the harem. I have read a hundred books on patience and still I am without it. What can I do! I must find a way to enjoy the love of this slender cypress, so that the desire of my body shall accord with the longing of my soul— and this must be done without his knowing.'

Then the sweet-voiced maids said: 'Do not grieve. To-night we will bring him here unknown to anyone, and even he will know nothing about it.'

Soon, one of the young girls went in secret to the slave and asked him, as if to play with him, to bring two cups of wine. Into one cup she threw a drug, contriving that he should drink it. He at once fell asleep, so that she was able to carry out her plan, and the youth of the silver breast remained without news of the two worlds.

When night came the maids of honour went softly to where he lay and put him on a litter and carried him to the princess. Then they sat him on a golden throne and placed a coronet of pearls on his head. At midnight, still a little drugged, he opened his eyes and saw a palace as fair as paradise, and around him were golden seats. The place was lighted by ten great candles perfumed with amber, and sweet aloe wood burned in pans. The maidens began to sing, but in such sweet strains that reason bade farewell to the spirit, and the soul to the body. Then the sun of wine went round to the light of the candles. Bewildered with the joy of his surroundings and dazzled by the beauty of the princess, the youth lost his wits. He was no longer really in this world nor was he in the other. With a heart full of love, and a body possessed with desire, amid these delights he fell into a state of ecstasy. His eyes were fastened on her beauty and his ears to the sound of the reed pipes. His nostrils took in the perfume of amber and the wine in his mouth became like liquid fire. The princess kissed him, and he shed tears of joy while she mingled hers with his. Sometimes she pressed sweet kisses on his mouth, sometimes they were tinged with salt; sometimes she ruffled his long hair, sometimes she lost herself in his eyes. He possessed her; and so they passed the time until the dawn appeared in the East. When morning Zephyr breathed the young slave became sad; but they sent him to sleep again and took him back to his quarters.

When he of the silver breast came to himself, without knowing why, he began to weep. One might say the thing was finished, so what was the good of crying out. He tore his clothes, pulled his hair and put earth on his head. Those about him asked why he was doing this, and what had happened. He said: 'It is impossible to describe what I have seen, no one else can ever see it except in a dream, for what has happened to me can never have happened to anyone before. Never was there a more astonishing mystery.'

Another said: 'Wake up, and tell us at least one of the hundred things that happened.' He replied: 'I am in a tumult because what I have seen has happened to me in another body. While hearing nothing I have heard everything, while seeing nothing I have seen everything.'

Another said: 'Have you lost your wits or have you just been dreaming?' 'Ah,' he said, 'I don't know if I was drunk or sober. What can be more puzzling than something which is neither revealed nor hidden. What I have seen I can never forget, yet I have no idea where it happened. For one whole night I revelled with a beauty who is without equal. Who and what she is I do not know. Only love remains, and that is all. But God knows the truth.'

THE MOTHER AND HER DEAD DAUGHTER

A passer-by, who saw a mother weeping over her daughter's grave said: 'This woman is superior to us men, for she knows whom she has lost and from whom she is parted. Happy the woman, or man, who knows whom he has lost, and for whom he weeps. As for me, though I sit in mourning and my tears flow like rain, I do not know for whom I weep. This woman carries away the ball of excellence from thousands like me, for she has found the perfume of the being she has lost.'.

THE LOST KEY

A Sufi heard a man cry out: 'Has anyone found a key? My door is locked and I stand in the dust of the road. If my door stays shut what shall I do?'

The Sufi said to him: 'Why do you worry? Since it is your door, stay near to it, even though it be shut. If you have patience to wait long enough no doubt someone will open it for you. Your situation is better than mine for I have neither door nor key. Would to God that I could find a door, open or shut.'

Man lives in a state of imagination, in a dream; no one sees things as they are. To him who says to you: 'What shall I do?' say to him: 'Do not do as you have always done; do not act as you have always acted.' He who enters the Valley of Astonishment has enough sorrow for a hundred worlds. For myself, I am bewildered and gone astray. Whither shall I direct my steps? Would to God I knew! But, remember; the groans of men bring down mercy.

THE PUPIL WHO SAW HIS TEACHER IN A DREAM

A pupil one night saw his dead teacher in a dream and said to him: 'Tell me what state you are in now. Since you went I have been lost in bewilderment, and burned up with grief.'

The pir replied: 'I am in such a state of amazement that I can only bite the back of my hand. I am in the pit, dumbfounded; and I have had more of a shock than ever I experienced in life.'

44

THE SEVENTH VALLEY
OR
THE VALLEY OF DEPRIVATION AND DEATH

The Hoopoe continued: 'Last of all comes the Valley of Deprivation and Death, which it is almost impossible to describe. The essence of this Valley is forgetfulness, dumbness, deafness and distraction; the thousand shadows which surround you disappear in a single ray of the celestial sun. When the ocean of immensity begins to heave, the pattern on its surface loses its form; and this pattern is no other than the world present and the world to come. Whoever declares that he does not exist acquires great merit. The drop that becomes part of this great ocean abides there for ever and in peace. In this calm sea, a man, at first, experiences only humiliation and overthrow; but when he emerges from this state he will understand it as creation, and many secrets will be revealed to him.

'Many beings have missed taking the first step and so have not been able to take the second—they can only be compared to minerals. When aloe wood and thorns are reduced to ashes they both look alike—but their quality is different. An impure object dropped into rose-water remains impure because of its innate qualities; but a pure object dropped in the ocean will lose its specific existence and will participate in the ocean and in its movement. In ceasing to exist separately it retains its beauty. It exists and non-exists. How can this be? The mind cannot conceive it.'

THE ADVICE OF NASSIR UDDIN

The beloved of Tūs, that ocean of spiritual secrets, said to one of his disciples: 'Melt yourself in the fire of love until you become as thin as a hair, then you will be fit to take your place among the locks of your beloved. If your eyes are turned towards the Way and if you are clear-seeing, then contemplate and ponder, hair by hair.

'He who leaves the world to follow this Way, finds death; he who finds death finds immortality. O my heart, if you have been turned inside out, cross the bridge Sirat and the burning fire; for when the oil in the lamp is burning it produces smoke as black as an old crow, but when it has been consumed by fire it ceases to have a coarse existence.

'If you wish to arrive at that high place first get rid of yourself; then go out from nothing as another Borak. Put on the khirka of nothingness and drink of the cup of annihilation, then cover your breast with the belt of belittlement

and put on your head the burnous of non-existence. Place
your foot in the stirrup of non-attachment, and urge your
useless steed towards the place where there is nothing. But
if there remains in you the least egoism the seven seas will
be, for you, full of adversity.'

STORY OF THE MOTHS

One night, the moths met together tormented by a desire to
be united to the candle. They said: 'We must send someone
who will bring us information about the object of our amorous
quest.' So one of them set off and came to a castle, and inside he saw the light of a candle. He returned, and according
to his understanding, reported what he had seen. But the
wise moth who presided over the gathering expressed the
opinion that he understood nothing about the candle. So
another moth went there. He touched the flame with the tip
of his wings, but the heat drove him off. His report being
no more satisfying than that of the first, a third went out.
This one, intoxicated with love, threw himself on the flame;
with his forelegs he took hold of the flame and united himself joyously with her. He embraced her completely and his
body became as red as fire. The wise moth, who was watching from far off, saw that the flame and the moth appeared to
be one, and he said: 'He has learnt what he wished to know;
but only he understands, and one can say no more.'

AN ILL-TREATED SUFI

A Sufi was sauntering leisurely along when he was struck
from behind. He turned round and said to the rogue who
had hit him: 'He whom you struck has been dead more than
thirty years.' The rogue replied: 'How can a dead man
speak? Be ashamed, you are not united to God. If you are
separated from him even by one hair it is as if you were a
hundred worlds away.'

When you are reduced to ashes, including your baggage, you will have not the least feeling of existence; but if there remains to you, as to Jesus, only a simple needle, a hundred thieves will lie in wait for you on the road. Although Jesus had thrown down his baggage, the needle was still able to scratch his face.

When existence disappears, neither riches nor empire, honours nor dignity, have any meaning.

THE PRINCE AND THE BEGGAR

There was once a king who had a son as charming as Joseph, full of grace and beauty. He was loved by everyone, and all who saw him would gladly have been the dust under his feet. If he went out at night, it was as if a new sun had risen over the desert. His eyes were the black narcissus, and when they glanced they set a world on fire. His smile scattered sugar, and wherever he walked a thousand roses bloomed, not waiting for the spring.

Now there was a simple dervish who had lost his heart to this young prince. Day and night he sat near the prince's palace, neither eating nor sleeping. His face became like yellow gold, and his eyes shed tears of silver, for his heart was cut in two. He would have died, but that from time to time he caught a glimpse of the young prince when he appeared in the bazaar. But how could such a prince comfort a poor dervish in this state? Yet the simple man, who was a shadow, a particle of an atom, wished to take the radiant sun on his breast.

One day when the prince was riding at the head of his attendants the dervish stood up and gave a cry and said: 'My reason has left me, my heart is consumed, I no longer have patience or strength to suffer,' and he beat his head on the ground in front of the prince. One of the courtiers wanted to have him killed, and went to the king. 'Sire,' he said, 'a libertine has fallen in love with your son.' The

king was very angry: 'Have this audacious scoundrel impaled,' he said. 'Bind him hand and foot and put his head
on a stake.' The courtier went at once to do his bidding.
They put a running noose on the neck of the beggar and
dragged him to the stake. No one knew what it was about
and no one interceded for him. When the wazir had had him
brought under the gibbet, the dervish gave a cry of grief and
said: 'For the love of God, give me a respite, so that at least
I can say a prayer under the gibbet.' This was allowed, and
the dervish prostrated himself and prayed: 'O God, since the
king has given orders for my death—I, who am innocent—
grant me, your ignorant servant, before I die, the good fortune to see only once the face of this young man, so that I
may offer myself as a sacrifice. O God, my King, you who
give ear to a thousand prayers, grant this last wish of mine.'

No sooner had the dervish uttered this prayer than the
arrow of his desire reached its mark. The wazir divined his
secret and took pity on him. He went to the king and ex-
plained the true state of things. At this the king became
thoughtful; then compassion filled his heart and he pardoned
the dervish, and said to the prince: 'Go and fetch this poor
man from under the gibbet. Be gentle with him and drink
with him, for he has tasted of your poison. Take him to your
garden and then bring him to me.'

The young prince, another Joseph, went at once—the sun
with a face of fire came face to face with an atom. This
ocean of beautiful pearls went to seek a drop of water. Beat
your head for joy, set your feet dancing, clap your hands!
But the dervish was in despair; his tears turned the dust to
mud and the world became heavy with his sighs. Even the
prince himself could not help but weep. When the dervish
saw his tears he said: 'O Prince, now you may take my life.'
And so saying, he gave up the ghost and died. When he
knew that he was united to his beloved no other desires were
left.

O you, who at once exist and are yet a non-entity, whose happiness is mingled with unhappiness, if you have never experienced unrest, how will you appreciate tranquillity? You stretch out your hand towards the lightning and are stopped by swept-up heaps of snow. Strive valiantly, burn reason, and give yourself up to folly. If you wish to use this alchemy reflect a little and, by my example, renounce yourself; withdraw from your wandering thoughts into your soul so that you may come to spiritual poverty. As for me, who am neither I nor not-I, I have strayed from myself, and I find no other remedy than despair.

QUESTION OF A DISCIPLE TO HIS SHAIKH

A man who was striving to overcome his weaknesses asked Nuri one day: 'How shall I ever be able to arrive at union with God?' Nuri replied: 'For this you must cross seven oceans of light and seven of fire, and travel a very long road. When you have crossed these twice seven oceans, a fish will draw you to him, such a fish that when he breathes he draws into his breast the first and the last. This marvellous fish has neither head nor tail; he holds himself in the middle of the ocean, quiet and detached; he sweeps away the two worlds, and he draws to himself all creatures without exception.'

45

ATTITUDE OF THE BIRDS

When the birds had listened to this discourse of the Hoopoe their heads drooped down, and sorrow pierced their hearts. Now they understood how difficult it would be for a handful of dust like themselves to bend such a bow. So great was their agitation that numbers of them died then and there. But others, in spite of their distress, decided to set out on the long road. For years they travelled over mountains and valleys, and a great part of their life flowed past on this journey. But how is it possible to relate all that happened to them? It would be necessary to go with them and see their difficulties for oneself, and to follow the wanderings of this long road. Only then could one realize what the birds suffered.

In the end, only a small number of all this great company arrived at that sublime place to which the Hoopoe had led them. Of the thousands of birds almost all had disappeared. Many had been lost in the ocean, others had perished on the summits of the high mountains, tortured by thirst; others had had their wings burnt and their hearts dried up by the fire of the sun; others were devoured by tigers and panthers; others died of fatigue in the deserts and in the wilderness, their lips parched and their bodies overcome by the heat; some went mad and killed each other for a grain of barley; others, enfeebled by suffering and weariness, dropped on the road unable to go further; others, bewildered by the things they saw, stopped where they were, stupefied; and many, who had started out from curiosity or pleasure, perished without an idea of what they had set out to find.

So then, out of all those thousands of birds, only thirty reached the end of the journey. And even these were bewildered, weary and dejected, with neither feathers nor wings. But now they were at the door of this Majesty that cannot be described, whose essence is incomprehensible— that Being who is beyond human reason and knowledge. Then flashed the lightning of fulfilment, and a hundred worlds were consumed in a moment. They saw thousands of suns each more resplendent than the other, thousands of moons and stars all equally beautiful, and seeing all this they were amazed and agitated like a dancing atom of dust, and they cried out: 'O Thou who art more radiant than the sun! Thou, who hast reduced the sun to an atom, how can we appear before Thee? Ah, why have we so uselessly endured

all this suffering on the Way? Having renounced ourselves
and all things, we now cannot obtain that for which we have
striven. Here, it little matters whether we exist or not.'

Then the birds, who were so disheartened that they resembled a cock half-killed, sank into despair. A long time
passed. When, at a propitious moment, the door suddenly
opened, there stepped out a noble chamberlain, one of the
courtiers of the Supreme Majesty. He looked them over and
saw that out of thousands only these thirty birds were left.

He said: 'Now then, O Birds, where have you come
from, and what are you doing here? What is your name? O
you who are destitute of everything, where is your home?
What do they call you in the world? What can be done with
a feeble handful of dust like you?'

'We have come,' they said, 'to acknowledge the Simurgh
as our king. Through love and desire for him we have lost
our reason and our peace of mind. Very long ago, when we
started on this journey, we were thousands, and now only
thirty of us have arrived at this sublime court. We cannot
believe that the King will scorn us after all the sufferings
we have gone through. Ah, no! He cannot but look on us
with the eye of benevolence!'

The Chamberlain replied: 'O you whose minds and
hearts are troubled, whether you exist or do not exist in the
universe, the King has his being always and eternally. Thousands of worlds of creatures are no more than an ant at his
gate. You bring nothing but moans and lamentations.
Return then to whence you came, O vile handful of earth!'

At this, the birds were petrified with astonishment. Nevertheless, when they came to themselves a little, they said:
'Will this great king reject us so ignominiously? And if he
really has this attitude to us may he not change it to one of
honour? Remember Majnun who said, "If all the people who
dwell on earth wished to sing my praises, I would not
accept them; I would rather have the insults of Laila. One

of her insults is more to me than a hundred compliments from another woman!"'

'The lightning of his glory manifests itself,' said the Chamberlain, 'and it lifts up the reason of all souls. What benefit is there if the soul be consumed by a hundred sorrows? What benefit is there at this moment in either greatness or littleness?'

The birds, on fire with love, said: 'How can the moth save itself from the flame when it wishes to be one with the flame? The friend we seek will content us by allowing us to be united to him. If now we are refused, what is there left for us to do? We are like the moth who wished for union with the flame of the candle. They begged him not to sacrifice himself so foolishly and for such an impossible aim, but he thanked them for their advice and told them that since his heart was given to the flame for ever, nothing else mattered.'

Then the Chamberlain, having tested them, opened the door; and as he drew aside a hundred curtains, one after the other, a new world beyond the veil was revealed. Now was the light of lights manifested, and all of them sat down on the masnad, the seat of the Majesty and Glory. They were given a writing which they were told to read through; and reading this, and pondering, they were able to understand their state. When they were completely at peace and detached from all things they became aware that the Simurgh was there with them, and a new life began for them in the Simurgh. All that they had done previously was washed away. The sun of majesty sent forth his rays, and in the reflection of each other's faces these thirty birds (si-murgh) of the outer world, contemplated the face of the Simurgh of the inner world. This so astonished them that they did not know if they were still themselves or if they had become the Simurgh. At last, in a state of contemplation, they realized that they were the Simurgh and that the Simurgh was the thirty birds. When they gazed at the Simurgh they

saw that it was truly the Simurgh who was there, and when
they turned their eyes towards themselves they saw that they
themselves were the Simurgh. And perceiving both at once,
themselves and Him, they realized that they and the Simurgh
were one and the same being. No one in the world has ever
heard of anything to equal it.

Then they gave themselves up to meditation, and after a
little they asked the Simurgh, without the use of tongues, to
reveal to them the secret of the mystery of the unity and
plurality of beings. The Simurgh, also without speaking,
made this reply: 'The sun of my majesty is a mirror. He who
sees himself therein sees his soul and his body, and sees them
completely. Since you have come as thirty birds, si-murgh,
you will see thirty birds in this mirror. If forty or fifty were
to come, it would be the same. Although you are now completely changed you see yourselves as you were before.

'Can the sight of an ant reach to the far-off Pleiades? And
can this insect lift an anvil? Have you ever seen a gnat seize
an elephant in its teeth? All that you have known, all that you
have seen, all that you have said or heard—all this is no
longer that. When you crossed the valleys of the Spiritual
Way and when you performed good tasks, you did all this
by my action; and you were able to see the valleys of my
essence and my perfections. You, who are only thirty birds,
did well to be astonished, impatient and wondering. But I
am more than thirty birds. I am the very essence of the
true Simurgh. Annihilate then yourselves gloriously and
joyfully in me, and in me you shall find yourselves.'

Thereupon, the birds at last lost themselves for ever in
the Simurgh—the shadow was lost in the sun, and that is all.

All that you have heard or seen or known is not even the
beginning of what you must know, and since the ruined
habitation of this world is not your place you must renounce it. Seek the trunk of the tree, and do not worry
about whether the branches do or do not exist.

IMMORTALITY AFTER ANNIHILATION

When a hundred thousand generations had passed, the mortal birds surrendered themselves spontaneously to total annihilation. No man, neither young nor old, can speak fittingly of death or immortality. Even as these things are far from us so the description of them is beyond all explanation or definition. If my readers wish for an allegorical explanation of the immortality that follows annihilation, it will be necessary for me to write another book. So long as you are identified with the things of the world you will not set out on the Path, but when the world no longer binds you, you enter as in a dream; but, knowing the end, you see the benefit. A germ is nourished among a hundred cares and loves so that it may become an intelligent and acting being. It is instructed and given the necessary knowledge. Then death comes and everything is effaced, its dignity is thrown down. This that was a being has become the dust of the street. It has several times been annihilated; but in the meanwhile it has been able to learn a hundred secrets of which previously it had not been aware, and in the end it receives immortality, and is given honour in place of dishonour. Do you know what you possess? Enter into yourself and reflect on this. So long as you do not realize your nothingness and so long as you do not renounce your self-pride, your vanity and your self-love, you will never reach the heights of immortality. On the Way you are cast down in dishonour and raised in honour.

And now my story is finished, I have nothing more to say.

EPILOGUE

O Attar! you have scattered on the world the contents of the vessel of the musk of secrets. The horizons of the world are full of your perfumes and lovers are disturbed because of you. Your verses are your seal; and they are known as Mantiq Uttair and Makamat Uttiyur. These conferences and talks and discourses of the birds are the stages of the way of bewilderment; or, one may say, they are the Diwan of Intoxication.

Enter into this diwan with love. When the Duldul of your love gallops and you desire something, act in conformity with your desire. Love is the remedy for all ills, and it is the remedy of the soul in the two worlds.

O you who have set out on the path of inner development, do not read my book only as a poetical work, or a book of magic, but read it with understanding; and for this a man must be hungry for something, dissatisfied with himself and this world.

He who has not smelt the perfume of my discourse has not found the way of lovers. But he who will read it with care will become active, and will be worthy to enter the Way of which I speak. Those of the outer world will be like drowned men as regards my discourse; but men of the inner world will understand its secrets. My book is the ornament of its time; it is at once a gift for distinguished men and a boon for the common. If a man as cold as ice reads this book he will shoot forth as fire out of the veil which hides the mystery from him. My writings have an astonishing peculiarity—they give more profit according to the manner in which they are read. If you ponder over them often they will benefit you more each time. The veil of this wife of the harem will be drawn aside for you only gradually in the place of honour and grace. I have scattered pearls from the ocean of contemplation; I am thereby acquitted, and this, my book, is the proof.

But if I praise myself too much, you may not approve; though he who is impartial will recognize my merit, for the light of my full moon is not hidden. If I am not remembered for myself I shall be remembered until the resurrection by the pearls of poetry that I have scattered on the heads of men. The cupolas of heaven will dissolve before this poem shall perish.

Reader, if you experience some well-being through having read this poem with attention, remember the writer in your prayers. I have strewn here and there roses from the garden. Remember me well, O my friends! Each teacher reveals his ideas in his own special way, and then he disappears. Like my predecessors I have revealed the bird of my soul to those who are asleep. Perhaps the sleep which fills your life has deprived you of this discourse; but, having met it, your soul will be awakened by the secret which it reveals.

And now my brain is smoked like a niche where stands a lamp. I have said to myself: 'O you who talk so much, instead of so much talking beat your head and search the secrets. What is the use of all these narrations to men corrupted with egoism. What can come out of hearts taken up with vanity and self-pride?'

If you wish the ocean of your soul to remain in a state of salutary movement you must die to all your old life, and then keep silence.

ATTAR

Farid ud-Din Abu Hāmid Muhammad ben Ibrāhīm was generally called Attar, the perfumer. Though little is known with certainty about his life, it seems that he was born in A.D. 1120 near Nishapūr in North-West Persia (the birthplace of Omar Khayyam). The date of his death is uncertain but is given as about A.D. 1230, so he lived to be a hundred and ten. Most of what is known about him is legendary, even his death at the hands of a soldier of Jenghis Khan. From his personal reminiscences scattered among his writings it seems that he spent thirteen years of his youth in Meshed. According to Dawlatshah, Attar was sitting one day with a friend at the door of his shop when a dervish came by, who looked in, smelt the sweet perfumes, then heaved a sigh and wept. Attar thought he was trying to arouse their pity and asked him to go away. The dervish said: 'Yes, there is nothing to prevent me leaving your door and saying farewell to this world. All I have is my worn-out khirka. But I grieve for you, Attar. How can you ever turn your mind to death and renounce all these worldly goods?' Attar replied that he hoped to end his life in poverty and contentment as a dervish. 'We shall see,' said the dervish, and thereupon lay down and died.

This made such an impression on Attar that he left his father's shop, became a pupil of the famous shaikh Bukn-ud-din, and began to study, in theory and practice, the Sufi system of ideas. For thirty-nine years he travelled in many countries, studying in monasteries and collecting the writings of devout Sufis, together with legends and stories. He then returned to Nishapūr where he lived for the remainder of his life. It was said that he had a deeper understanding of Sufi ideas than anyone of his time. He composed about two hundred thousand verses and many works in prose. He lived before Jalāl-uddin Rūmī. A Sufi being asked who of these two understood most, said: 'Rūmī flew up to the heights of perfection like an eagle in the twinkling of an eye; Attar reached the same place by creeping like an ant.' Rūmī said: 'Attar is the soul itself.'

Garcin de Tassy relates that in 1862 Nicholas Khanikoff discovered a stone outside Nishapūr, which had been erected some-
time between 1469 and 1506 (some two hundred and fifty years
after Attar's death) on which was engraved an inscription in
Persian. Tassy's translation of this into French I render as follows:

God is Eternal
In the name of God
The Compassionate the Merciful

Here in this garden of a lower Eden, Attar perfumed the soul
of the humblest of men. This is the tomb of a man so eminent
that the dust stirred by his feet would have served as collyrium
to the eye of the firmament; of the illustrious shaikh Attar Farid,
of whom the saints were disciples; of this excellent perfumer whose
breath embalmed the world from one Kāf to another. In his shop,
that nest of angels, the firmament is as a phial of pellets perfumed
with citron. The earth of Nishapūr will be renowned until the
day of resurrection because of this illustrious man. The mine of
his gold is found at Nishapūr for he was born at Zarwand in the
district of Gurgān. He lived at Nishapūr for eighty-two years, of
which thirty-two were passed in tranquillity. In the year of the
Hijra 586 [1190] he was pursued by the sword of the army which
devoured everything. Farid perished in the time of Hulākū Khan,
being martyred in the massacre which then took place . . . May
God, the Most High, refresh his soul! Increase, O Lord, his merit.

The tombstone of this eminent man was placed here in the
reign of the King of the World, His Majesty Sultan Abū Igazī
Hussein . . .

The rest of the inscription is in praise of the Sultan. There
seems not to be any contemporary written record of how, when
or where he died or was buried.

A NOTE ON THE SUFIS

The name is derived from suf, wool—woollen robes of ascetics. The Sufis follow the inner teaching of the Korān. Together with a system of ideas based on the precepts of their sacred book, they have a practical method for working on themselves, which is taught orally. By means of exercises, postures, and dances, the forces of man, which are continually being diverted away from himself, may be used and converted for inner development and the increasing of consciousness. The aim and end is union of the soul with God. There may be moments of foretaste of this— moments of revelation and ecstasy—'gifts', as they are called, but perfection, union with God, must be worked for; there must be constant striving.

There is one God. All things are in Him and He is in all things. All things, visible and invisible, are emanations of Him. Religions, in themselves, are not important, though they may serve to lead men to Reality. Good and Evil, as we understand them, do not really exist, for everything proceeds from the One Being, God; at the same time, there is real good and real evil. Man is not free in his actions; he has no free-will, though this may be achieved through striving in the right way. He is turned this way and that way by interior and exterior forces—the sport of every wind that blows. Union is attained through two forms of renunciation and detachment: our own desires, vanities, day-dreams, on the one hand; and the things of the world on the other—love of power, fame, riches and honours. But prayer and fasting also can be a great hindrance: one can become identified with any- thing. A Sufi, however, should not renounce necessaries and should not retire from the world. He must be in it but not of it. It is a great blessing to have what is necessary for the physical body. Sex in itself was not an occasion for sin, as it became in orthodox Christianity, but a prized possession. The meaning and use of the sex force was understood. As Orage points out in his essay 'On Love', 'The chastity of the senses [in ancient times] was taught in early childhood. Eroticism thereby became an art in the highest form the world has seen. Its faint echoes are to be found in Persian and Sufi literature today.'

The soul (in the sense of that higher part of man which longs for perfection) existed before the body and is confined in it as in a cage. Human life is a journey which is made in stages; and the seeker after God a traveller, who must make great efforts to overcome his weaknesses and faults, and to obtain true knowledge and understanding.

Its followers say that Sufism has always existed under various names; and that the system and method, in different forms, was known to the Egyptians, Hindus, Buddhists, Jews, Greeks, and early Christians—in fact, to all of the great religions in their origins. It exists in the West today.

Only the fellowship of those who have reached a certain state of development can set the traveller on the path. Provided he has the ableness for discipline and effort, a single day—even a single hour, in the society of men of understanding is of more value than years of asceticism and exterior forms of worship.

Among the rules for pupils in the presence of a teacher are the following: 'Pay attention and speak little. Don't answer questions not addressed to you; but if asked, answer promptly, and don't be ashamed to say "I don't know". Don't dispute for the sake of disputation. Don't boast before your elders. Don't seek the highest place. Don't be over-ceremonious. Obey all ordinary conventions, and conform to the wishes of others so long as they are not against your inner convictions. Don't make a practice of anything, except it is a religious duty or useful to others, since it may become an idol.'

The Sufis say that almost everyone is born with possibilities for inner development but that his parents and those around him make him a Jew, a Christian, a Hindu, or a Magician, and he soon acquires prejudices and accepts what others say with no regard to his own experience or reasoning, and this becomes a stumbling-block. When a 'believer' dies—one who has worked on himself—his soul goes to that heaven which corresponds to the state to which it has been perfected. But, however much 'knowledge' a man has, unless he has examined himself, and confessed to himself that really he understands nothing, all that he has acquired will be as 'the wind in his hand'.

GLOSSARY

ABRAHAM, IBRAHIM: One of the six great prophets. Nimrod had him thrown into a fiery furnace but he was rescued by the Angel Gabriel and the fire changed into a garden of roses. Nimrod made war on Abraham, but his army was defeated by swarms of gnats, one of which crept into Nimrod's brain; he who wished to be Lord of all was punished by the smallest of creatures.

ABRAHAH: Also called Azaz and Tharé. Father of Abraham. An idolater and fire-worshipper.

ADAM: Muslims consider him to be the first prophet, the 'chosen of God', Khalif of God on earth. The first man. According to Muslims, wheat was the forbidden food which Adam ate in Paradise.

ALAST: The first word of a passage in the Korān, 'Am I not your Lord?' The words addressed to human souls contained in Adam, who replied 'Yes'.

ANGELS: Are thought to be of a simple substance. Four are archangels: Gabriel, the angel of Revelations; Michael, the patron of the Israelites; Israfil, who will sound the trumpet on the last day; Azrael, the angel of death. Munkir and Nakir examine the dead in their graves. There are many others.

ANT: Guided Solomon across the desert.

ARK: Consisted of three stories—the lowest for beasts, the next for humans, the top for birds.

BEARD: By Muslims regarded as the badge of dignity and manhood. Hence: 'By the beard of the Prophet.'

BIRD OF THE SOUL: Joined the soul to the body, body to spirit.

BIRDS: Muslims believe that all kinds of birds (and many beasts) have a language by which they speak to each other. King Solomon was taught the language of the birds.

BISMILLAH: In the name of God.

BORAK, BURAQ: The Bright One. The animal on which Muhummad made the journey at night, the Mi'rāj. A white animal smaller than a horse, with wings.

BRIDGE: 'Across the water', for the Israelites over the Red Sea.

CAT: A cat woke Muhammad when it was time for prayer. Abu Qutadah said, 'Cats are not impure, they keep watch round about us'.

DANG: Quarter of a dinar.

DEATH: The Korān teaches that the hour of death is fixed for every living creature. 'If God were to punish men for their wrong-doing he would not leave a single human being on earth, but he gives them a respite; and when their time comes they can neither delay it for a single hour, nor can they hasten it.'

DERVISH: Persian, from 'dar', a door, so Darwesh. Begging from door to door. Arabic, faquir—the poor in spirit. They follow the teachings of the Sufis. There are different orders of dervishes.

DEVIL: Shaitan, the Opposer. Iblis, The Wicked One. Shaitan also denotes one who is far from the truth; and Iblis, one who is without hope. Muhammad said: 'There is not one of you but has an angel and a devil appointed over him.' The Companions asked: 'Do you include yourself?' He said: 'Yes, for me also, but God has given me the victory over the devil and he does not direct me except in what is good. Not one of the sons of Adam, except Mary and her son Jesus, but is touched by the devil at birth—hence his cries.'

DIMPLE: The allusion is often to a well or spring.

DINAR: Gold coin worth about two pounds today.

DOGS: Unclean animals to Muslims, though hunting with trained dogs is permitted. A dog is able to see Azrael, the angel of death.

EATING: Muslims are enjoined to eat in the name of God. The devil has power over food that is eaten without remembering God. When a man remembers the name of God, and remembers himself, at meal times, the devil says to his demons: 'This is no place for us: nor is there any food.'

FOUR GOLDEN WALLS: Points of the compass.

GENII: Good and evil spirits. Among them are Janns, Jinn, Shaitans, Ifrits and Marids. The evil Jinn are called by the Persians, Deves.

GOD: There are a hundred names, or attributes of God. The first and last being Allah.

GREEN: For the Persian the colour of heaven is green.

HEAVEN: The firmament. Distinct from Paradise, the abode of bliss. There are seven heavens, and seven stages or seven paths in Heaven. Muhammad passed through the seven during the Mi'rāj.

HELL: The Fire. Hell has seven doors or divisions. One is Jahannan, the purgatorial hell.

HIJRA: 'Migration.' Flight of Muhammad from Mecca. Also 'fleeing from sin'.

HOOPOE: Hūdhūd, from its call. When Solomon had finished the temple he went on a pilgrimage to Mecca and from there to Arabia Felix. Needing water he called the Hoopoe, for she was able to discover water underground, and when she marked the place with her beak, the demons drew the water. The Hoopoe carried the letter from Solomon to Balkis, the Queen of Sheba. Reviewing the birds, Solomon said: 'I do not see the Hudhud. Is she then among the absent?' A mark on her beak resembles the Persian character 'Bismillah'. Her 'crown of glory' is her crest. When its mate dies it does not take a new one; also, it cares for its parents. Muhammad forbade his people to kill it.

HOSPITALITY: 'Show kindness to your parents, to your kindred, to orphans, to your neighbours, to the companion who is strange, and to the son of the road', Korān.

HUMA OR HUMAY: Bearded griffon. Largest of birds of prey in the Old World. Carries off bones of dead animals and smashes them against rocks for food. The shadow of a huma falling on a person's head is a sign that he will be raised to a throne.

IDIOT: Arabic, Madjnun. A person whose mind is in heaven, his body on earth. Whatever an idiot of God may do it does not affect his sanctity. In early English the Apostles and simple people were spoken of as idiots. 'Holy and innocent idiots', Jeremy Taylor. Greek, 'a private person'. In some esoteric teachings: one who is freeing himself from inner and outer attachments. There are stages of this. Also used in the other sense: a fool, lunatic, impostor.

ISPAND: Herb, perhaps mustard, burnt at births and marriages to avert the evil eye.

ISHMAEL: The progenitor of the Arab race, an inspired prophet. Said to have been offered as a sacrifice, not Isaac.

JESUS: Muhammad speaks of him as Son of Mary, the Messiah, Word of God, Word of Truth, Messenger from God. He was not crucified, but a substitute was put on the cross. Taken up to the seventh heaven, and by accident a needle and broken pitcher with him, against God's command forbidding earthly things, for which he was brought down to the fourth heaven. But he will stay there in glory and come again at the last day. Often referred to as a fish, also by Attar. Greek for fish is ΙΧΘΥΣ the initial letters of Ιησους Χριστος Θεου Υιος Σωτηρ Jesus Christ Son of God Saviour.

JEWS: Were favoured by God. In possession of divine teaching, which they have forsaken.

JIHAD: An effort, a striving. Sufis say there are two Jihads or warfares: the greater against our own faults and weaknesses, the lesser against the infidels.

JOSEPH: Son of Jacob. An inspired prophet. Thrown into a well. After he was sold to the Egyptians his master's wife Zulaikha fell in love with him and he with her. But because he would not yield she had him imprisoned. When her husband died she and Joseph were married and had two sons. One of the great love stories of the East is 'Joseph and Zulaikha'.

KA'ABA: Cube. The cube-shaped stone building in the centre of the Mosque at Mecca. Contains the Hajaru'l-Aswad, or black stone which came from heaven white but has become black because of the sins of those who have touched it.

KĀF: Mountain range which surrounds the earth.

AL KAUSAR: 'Abundance.' A pool in Muhammad's Paradise.

KHIRKA: Mantle of the dervishes, made of pieces and patches.

AL KHIZR: Said to have lived in the time of Abraham, is still alive, for he drank of the water of life and thereby obtained immortality.

KNEE: See 'Shaikh and the old woman'. Allusion to a posture of the Sufis.

KORAH: Numbers, Chap. 16.

MAHMŪD: A.D. 969–1030. One of the most famous of Musulmān rulers. His capital was at Nishapūr; and his court at Gaznā was the resort of poets, artists and the learned.

MAHRĀM: A near relative, whom it is not lawful to marry; so, an intimate.

MASNAD: Seat of royalty, on which there is room for several persons.

MAJNŪN: 'Possessed by a Jinni.' His passion for Laïla is one of the great love stories of Persia. They fell in love at first sight but her father made her marry another man. Majnūn spent the rest of his life half-naked, catching rare glimpses of Laïla, and writing poems to her. Sufi writers use the story as a similitude for the man who gives up everything to be united to God.

MIHRĀB: Niche in a Mosque pointing to Mecca.

MULE: Allusion to a custom in the East whereby women would convey letters or small precious objects secretly in the animal's vagina. In Persia, thieves were marked on the shoulder.

NĀFS: Has several aspects. One, the forces that move man through his centres. Another, the denying part.

OBOL: A small coin in use in the Near East and Europe in early times. Worth about a threepenny bit.

PHOENIX: Its 'trumpet' is an allusion to the last day.

PĪR: An elder. Religious leader. Old man.

PIT: Dry cisterns and wells were used as prisons.

QALANDARS: An order of dervishes in Persia and Arabia whose object is perpetual wandering. Founded by Qalandar Yūsuf al Andalusī of Spain.

RUINS: Muslims often concealed themselves there to drink the forbidden wine.

SHAIKH: Pronounced as spelt. A superior of an order of dervishes, or monastery. A venerable old man. Head of a family or tribe.

SIMURGH: Sen-murgh, the Great Bird. In the Mahabharata, Garuda. There are two Simurghs. One lives on Mt. Elbruz in the Caucasus, far from man. Its nest is of pillars of ebony, sandal, and aloe wood. It has the gift of speech and its feathers possess magical properties. It is a guardian of heroes, a symbol of God. The other one is a horrible monster which also lives on a mountain, but it resembles a black cloud.

SIRAT: The Right Way, True Path. A bridge across the infernal abyss. It is finer than a hair, sharper than a sword, beset with briars and thorns. The good will pass over safely but the wicked will fall into the depths.

SOLOMON: There is a legend that the Jinn robbed Solomon of his seal, and so deprived him of his power for forty days. The ring was found in a fish and restored to Solomon together with his power. It is also said that later Solomon threw the ring into the sea so that none should learn the secret of his power. He is alluded to by Attar as 'a mineral in the earth'.

SOUL: Attar sometimes uses the word in two senses. One, of man's higher part, the other, of the lower. In this book the soul is used for the higher, divine part; and 'body of desire' for the lower.

SPIDER: Shielded Muhammad by spinning a web across the entrance to a cave in which he was hiding.

TWO LETTERS: 'With two letters he created . . .' Letters Kāf and Nūn, forming Kūn, meaning 'Be'.

WAGTAIL: There is a play on words in the original Persian. Wagtail, mūcicha; Moses, Mūca; shawm, mūcichar.

ZIKR OR DHIKR: 'Remembering.' Remembering God, remembering oneself. The name of various ceremonies practised by the different orders of dervishes, consisting of prayers, dances, postures and so on, which were (and still are in certain places) exercises for inner development and the increasing of consciousness. Some of the dances were scripts for the imparting of knowledge. 'Ho Yah', 'Hoo Yah', 'O Heh'—'O God', is an exclamation of dervishes in some of their religious exercises. Also 'Ya Hai', 'O thou Living'.

ZUNNAR: A girdle. The belt worn by Christians and Jews. A term used by Sufis for sincerity in the path of religion. Also used to denote exterior practices of religion.